DISCARD

YOU SHOULD
BE SO LUCKY

You Should Be So Lucky

A NEW COMEDY BY
Charles Busch

GARDEN CITY, NEW YORK

Photos of the 1994 Primary Stages production by Andrew Leynse.
Design by Maria Chiarino
Manufactured in the United States of America
ISBN 1-56865-000-0

YOU SHOULD BE SO LUCKY opened in New York City on November 2, 1994. It was produced by Primary Stages, Casey Childs, Artistic Director in association with The Herrick Theatre Foundation. It was directed by Kenneth Elliott. The Production Stage Manager was John Frederick Sullivan. The cast (in order of appearance) was as follows:

Mr. Rosenberg	Stephen Pearlman
Christopher	Charles Busch
Polly	Nell Campbell
Walter	Matthew Arkin
Lenore	Julie Halston
Wanda Wang	Jennifer Kato

THE TIME: The present.

SETTING: A small railroad apartment in Greenwich Village. We are in the living room. A door up left leads outside and an archway up right, covered with a curtain of beads, leads off to a kitchen and bedroom. The decor is a mad combination of Chinese kitsch and Art Nouveau, all collected for next to nothing at flea markets. The walls are crowded with antique fans and Samurai swords. An old-fashioned barber chair is down right. The dominating feature of the room is a large Victorian sofa, smothered in heavily fringed velvet throws and pillows. Once one becomes accustomed to the fake opulence of the room, one notices the cracked, moldy walls and half-stripped woodwork.

It's midafternoon on a hot summer day.

TO KEN ELLIOTT

ACT
ONE

ACT
ONE

ACT ONE

Scene One

Mr. Rosenberg enters from the archway with an old-fashioned ice pack. He is a tall, imposing man in his sixties, dressed in a beautifully tailored suit. He projects an elegant elder-statesman quality and also a cuddly, grandfatherly warmth. His speech still retains a trace of his Lower East Side roots.

ROSENBERG (*talking to someone in the kitchen*): This is really quite a place, (*up center, to himself*) quite a place. So many things. (*To himself*) What does it remind me of? A whorehouse in Shanghai or my Aunt Basha's apartment in Riverdale? (*To the person in the kitchen*) Please accept this in the spirit in which it's intended, Christopher, I realize I'm a complete stranger, but you really should find yourself a good plasterer. These walls. . . . (*Muttering to himself*) *Ah zoy tzebrachn mir kin platzn.* (*To the person in the kitchen*) The floors are good floors—(*to himself*) they could use a good sanding. (*Crossing to window*) You should have your landlord replace these old windows. You'd be amazed at how much you'll save on heat in the winter. (*Looking out the window*) And that stoop out front—that's an accident waiting to happen. Keep in mind these are just suggestions.

(Christopher enters from the kitchen holding a tray of tea things. He is a very boyish young man in his early thirties. He is an eccentric blend of intense timidity and equally intense enthusiasm)

CHRISTOPHER (*putting tea tray on the coffee table*): Here's your tea, Mr. Rosenberg. You look much better. You really gave me a fright. (*He sits and begins pouring tea*)

ROSENBERG: I'm fine, I'm fine. You know, Christopher, this could be a very charming apartment. High ceilings.

CHRISTOPHER: I really should fix it up. It has great possibilities. I'm mad about the windows. But I never know how long I'm going to stay.

ROSENBERG: How long have you been here?

CHRISTOPHER: Twelve years. Sugar?

ROSENBERG: Please.

CHRISTOPHER (*picking up a sugar packet and emptying its contents into a cup*): It's been quite a while since I've entertained.

ROSENBERG: How long's it been?

CHRISTOPHER: Twelve years. Milk?

ROSENBERG: No, thank you.

CHRISTOPHER (*handing him the cup of tea*): Here you go.

ROSENBERG (*accepting it, he stirs and notices something on the rim*): This is a fine piece of china. You really should get that chip repaired.

CHRISTOPHER: I really should. It hasn't been broken very long.

ROSENBERG (*cautiously*): How long?

CHRISTOPHER: Twelve years. Cracker? (*Holds up a package of saltines*)

ROSENBERG: No, thank you. (*Drinking*)

CHRISTOPHER: How are you feeling?

ROSENBERG: Much better. It was just a little dizziness.

CHRISTOPHER: You blacked out completely.

ROSENBERG: This humidity is deadly for senior citizens.

CHRISTOPHER: You know, maybe you should see a doctor. We're very close to St. Vincent's.

ROSENBERG: I'm fine. I'm just lucky that I didn't hit my head on the pavement. Christopher, you're a true Samaritan; bringing me into your apartment, a complete and total stranger. Please, let me give you something for your generosity. (*He puts his tea cup down on the coffee table and takes out his wallet*)

CHRISTOPHER: Please, put that away.

ROSENBERG (*handing him money*): There's a marvelous seafood restaurant on Hudson Street. Have a surf and turf on me.

CHRISTOPHER: You'll hurt my feelings if you go on like that.

ROSENBERG: You're quite a kid. (*Putting the money away*)

CHRISTOPHER: My mother was a nurse. I guess I take after her.

ROSENBERG (*seeing a framed photo on the table*): Are these your parents?

CHRISTOPHER: Yes.

ROSENBERG: A handsome couple.

CHRISTOPHER: That was their wedding photo.

ROSENBERG: Are they still living?

CHRISTOPHER: No, they both died when I was very young. They were both extraordinary people. My mother was not only a nurse but a poet, a flautist and a champion figure skater.

ROSENBERG: Oh my.

CHRISTOPHER (*picking up and displaying a tray table*): These are her medals. And my father was a horseman, a puppeteer and a piano tuner. (*Picking up an object from the sofa table just above sofa*) This was his pitch pipe.

ROSENBERG: Are you musical?

CHRISTOPHER: Oh no. I'm afraid I didn't inherit much from them. Even the clutter I found for myself.

ROSENBERG (*crossing to barber chair*): This is a nice old-fashioned piece of furniture. Are you a barber?

CHRISTOPHER (*meeting him at barber chair*): I'm an electrologist. (*Rosenberg looks puzzled*) An electrologist. I remove unwanted hair from people.

ROSENBERG: Really? You went to school for this?

CHRISTOPHER: Oh yes. I'm a trained professional.

ROSENBERG: Is it painful, this . . . plucking?

CHRISTOPHER: More discomfort than pain. And we do not pluck. We do not pluck. I just get livid when ignorant people dismiss us as mere pluckers. (*Showing him a chart, just above barber chair*) I have a needle with an electric charge that destroys the papilla, the seed of the hair directly below the root. I can show you before-and-after photos of my clients. You probably wouldn't be interested.

ROSENBERG: No, I would. Please. (*Christopher hesitates*) No, I really would. Show me.

CHRISTOPHER: Okay. (*Christopher crosses tentatively to desk*)

ROSENBERG: I admire a fellow who's enthusiastic about his work.

CHRISTOPHER (*putting down tea cup, he opens top drawer of desk and rifles through a bunch of papers*): I can be almost obsessive. My sister Polly says I'm a natural electrologist because I have a great need to smooth things over. Here they are. (*Takes out an envelope with photos and crossing to better light by window, urging Rosenberg to join him*) This is Miss Fernandez. She's from New Rochelle. Here she is before.

ROSENBERG: Oh my, the poor woman. We used to call those mutton chop whiskers.

CHRISTOPHER: It was a challenge. Even then I thought she was a handsome woman. When she wore black, she looked rather like Johnny Cash. (*Finding another photo*) Here she is several months later. Isn't she gorgeous?

ROSENBERG: Sort of a prettier Anthony Quinn.

CHRISTOPHER (*abruptly putting photos back in envelope*): I'm sorry if I fail to find that amusing. We worked very hard for nearly a year clearing up her . . . um, whiskers.

ROSENBERG: I'm sorry for being flip.

CHRISTOPHER: If you could have seen her expression of pure joy when we finally got rid of her mustache. Her face is my greatest achievement, my *Schindler's List*.

ROSENBERG: You're very deep.

CHRISTOPHER: Not really. It's just that my superficiality is rather complex. (*He returns photos to desk drawer*)

ROSENBERG: You know, Christopher, I might be in the market for your services. It's this little bit on my back and shoulders. A light dusting that could use some electrolysizing. Do you think that's terribly vain or womanish of me?

CHRISTOPHER: *Au contraire*, Mr. Rosenberg. I applaud your vanity. Bravo. (*Striking an effeminate pose*) There is nothing effeminate about good grooming.

ROSENBERG: I'm thinking about making a few changes in my life. My wife died just over two years ago. She was a remarkable woman. We had a forty-two year romance. Are you married?

CHRISTOPHER: No.

ROSENBERG: Y'ever been married? Engaged?

CHRISTOPHER: No. I'm afraid I'm the cat that walks alone.

ROSENBERG: My friend, you're missing out on something.

CHRISTOPHER: I am passionate about my work *and* my hobbies. (*Pointing to shelf above desk*) I paint goblin faces on dried yams.

ROSENBERG: Yams? Well, um, recently I told myself, "Enough already, stop with the grieving, get on with your life." Perhaps I'm a fool, but I thought I'd try dating again. Perhaps I should make a few improvements to give myself a more attractive appearance. How much do you charge?

CHRISTOPHER. Forty dollars for an hour's session. That's pretty standard. You can check if you want, but I don't bargain. I'm a trained professional. (*Insecure*) You think that's too much?

ROSENBERG: No, no. I thought it would be more. I have no plans for the rest of the afternoon. Could we start right now? Unless you have other appointments.

CHRISTOPHER (*retrieving his appointment book from desk*): I may. Let me see. Hmmm. (*It's empty*) I think I can fit you in.

(*There's loud pounding on the front door*)

POLLY (*outside*): Christopher! Open up! I need you! I know you're in there!

CHRISTOPHER: My sister Polly.

ROSENBERG (*getting up*): You'd better answer it. We'll do this some other time.

CHRISTOPHER: No, you'll never come back. And it's been so slow.

POLLY (*outside*): Please let me in!

ROSENBERG: She sounds like she's in trouble.

CHRISTOPHER: She's an unemployed actress. Her entire union's in trouble.

POLLY (*outside*): Christopher, please!

ROSENBERG: Open the door.

(*Christopher crosses left and up, opens the door and Polly falls in. A flamboyant, jazzy redhead. She lugs in some suitcases, shopping bags, a hatbox and a dead-looking plant. She immediately drops everything, save the plant, which she deposits on the desk. She speaks in a lovely British accent*)

POLLY: Thank God!

CHRISTOPHER: What is all this?

POLLY: The effects of a lifetime. (*Seeing Rosenberg*) Please sir, whoever you are, move a little to the right. (*Crossing to sofa*) I need to fling myself on that divan. I can't even fling. I'm quite beyond the dramatic gesture. (*In a fit of tears, she throws herself dramatically onto the sofa*)

CHRISTOPHER: Polly, this is Mr. Rosenberg.

POLLY (*not yet recovered*): Yes.

CHRISTOPHER: What happened?

POLLY (*slowly sitting up*): Sam threw me out. Out into the streets. Look at me, once a figure of glamour, now but a husk of a woman.

CHRISTOPHER (*leaning on sofa arm*): Polly, you must get your name on a lease. You can't go on like this.

POLLY: What do you mean? Never before has a man tossed my clothes out of an eighth-floor window. No, I should never have involved myself with someone so much younger.

CHRISTOPHER: And so volatile.

POLLY: You don't know how many nights I feared for my life. He can't accept that he's a failure. A failed playwright.

CHRISTOPHER: He's only twenty-four.

POLLY: He failed before he began!

CHRISTOPHER: I hadn't heard from you in a month.

POLLY: Darling, I was his prisoner in the San Remo. I might as well have been in Kuwait. The whole situation came to a boil when I flung his damned manuscript into the fire and watched it burn.

ROSENBERG (*sitting next to her*): You destroyed his play? I can see why he was miffed.

CHRISTOPHER: I hope it was only a one-act.

POLLY: It was a verse trilogy. The play was his child and I gladly watched it turn to ashes. Burn! Burn! I'm burning your child!

CHRISTOPHER: Polly played Hedda Gabler in Tulsa. I saw it. She was absolutely brilliant.

POLLY: My greatest fan.

ROSENBERG: Polly, you sound British.

POLLY: Well, I've lived for many years in England.

CHRISTOPHER: She studied at The Royal Academy and played one season in Manchester.

POLLY: Two seasons.

ROSENBERG (*to Chris*): Pardon me for saying this, but, you talk a little funny too.

CHRISTOPHER: I spent a long weekend with her.

ROSENBERG: Where are you both from originally?

CHRISTOPHER and POLLY: Albuquerque.

CHRISTOPHER: Polly, what are you going to do?

POLLY: Start again. Somewhere. Somehow. Frankly, I'm at your mercy.

CHRISTOPHER: It's a very small apartment.

POLLY: But I can make myself useful. I can do manicures and pedicures. It'll be better than me paying you rent. (*To Rosenberg*) Darling, let me see those cuticles.

CHRISTOPHER: Leave him alone. (*Picking up her luggage*) What can I say? I guess you've already moved in. Is this it?

POLLY: My entire world.

CHRISTOPHER (*noticing the plant on the desk*): Why'd you save that dead plant?

POLLY: That plant is far from dead. That plant is nesting.

CHRISTOPHER: It's an amaryllis?!

POLLY: The most glorious amaryllis. And it's due to bloom some time early fall. We have to set it in the bottom of a closet in the dark. I promise you, Christopher, I will have my own place before it blooms. (*Christopher exits with her luggage through the archway*) I mean, really, how long can it be before I land a starring role in a hit play? Mr. Rosenberg, what line of work are you in?

ROSENBERG: I'm in the financial world. I advise.

POLLY (*flirtatiously*): How I wish I had some assets you could advise me on.

CHRISTOPHER (*re-entering*): You're sitting on one. Don't take her seriously. She's always acting. (*Slightly offended, POLLY turns away*)

ROSENBERG: Frankly, I was enjoying the performance.

POLLY (*turning back and taking a deep curtsy*): Thank you.

CHRISTOPHER (*picking up his cup of tea*) Polly gets everything she wants simply through charm. I've been her slave all my life.

ROSENBERG: I can see why. She's a very vivacious young lady.

CHRISTOPHER: And totally selfish and egocentric.

POLLY: I've had to make my own way in the world. I've had a less than spectacular career in the theatre and it's left its scars.

CHRISTOPHER: Oh, you were this way when you used to drown my dolls in the bathtub.

POLLY: I didn't.

CHRISTOPHER: Have you forgotten "Titanic Barbie"?

POLLY: Well, I always resuscitated her. Now I need to do the same for you.

CHRISTOPHER: Here we go.

POLLY: It's kismet that brought me here. You need me. You live like some pathetic eccentric immersed in a world of shadows and dusty corners. (*"Displaying" Chris*) Meet my brother, Miss Havisham.

CHRISTOPHER: You really have a lot of nerve barging in here and asking for my help and then criticizing me. I have a very full life. I provide a service that frees people from society's unjust stigma against excessive body hair. I have a wonderful family of loyal friends.

POLLY: Oh cool down. You're so touchy about the slightest bit of criticism. (*Crossing to Rosenberg at sofa*) Mr. Rosenberg, my brother and I are both classic examples of adult children of alcoholics.

CHRISTOPHER: Who was an alcoholic?

POLLY: Mother was. He's morbidly obsessed with our parents, but knows nothing about them.

CHRISTOPHER: But Polly—

POLLY: Mother drank like a flounder. Believe me, Chris, I know a lot about this. Adult children of alcoholics find it impossible to complete things. I've never seen you finish a crossword puzzle or a plate of escargot. Classic.

CHRISTOPHER: But Mother wasn't an alcoholic.

POLLY: How would you know? You were only nine when she fell out the window. I was eleven and keenly perceptive.

CHRISTOPHER: But Polly . . .

POLLY: Mother was a drunk! (*Charging at him*) Don't argue with me! And you're going to follow in her wobbling footsteps.

CHRISTOPHER: I never have more than one Pimm's Cup.

POLLY: Trust me. In time, you will drink more. An alcoholic drinks out of loneliness and frustration.

CHRISTOPHER: Are you finished?

POLLY: I'm just getting revved up.

CHRISTOPHER: Mr. Rosenberg, I'm really sorry. This strange woman has some fixation that I'm her brother. Why don't you go into the bedroom and change. There's a kimono on a hook inside the armoire.

ROSENBERG: (*Repeating*) In the armoire. (*He exits*)

CHRISTOPHER (*picking up tea tray*): Polly, you really are wrong. I'm not lonely. I do have friends. Close friends. Norma Leeds for one. (*Depositing tea tray on sofa table*)

POLLY: She's ninety-two and hasn't spoken since her last stroke.

CHRISTOPHER: Um . . . Steven Deautsch.

POLLY: He's ten years old. Who do you think you are? Michael Jackson?

CHRISTOPHER (*removing a decorative lamp shade from the gooseneck surgical lamp above chair*): Roger Bernstein's my age.

POLLY: I'm surprised you don't count him as three people.

CHRISTOPHER: He's on a different medication now. (*Putting lamp shade on stool below archway*)

POLLY: These aren't friends. These are cases.

CHRISTOPHER (*impatiently; opening electrolysis cabinet on wall behind chair*): Polly, I have work to do.

POLLY (*indicating plant on desk*): Christopher, look at that plant. You are that amaryllis.

CHRISTOPHER (*wearily; turning barber chair to face upstage and adjusting seat back into a prone position*): Oh Polly . . .

POLLY: You are that amaryllis. You've been in decades of withdrawal, alone in a dark closet.

CHRISTOPHER: This symbolism is really hokey. (*He turns on the electrolysis machine. We hear a hum*)

POLLY: I'm an actress, not a playwright.

CHRISTOPHER (*grabbing a length of paper towel from underneath cabinet and placing it over the barber chair*): I was doing so fine . . .

POLLY: No you weren't. Christopher, you have no life. You have excuses to be busy.

CHRISTOPHER (*at the end of his rope; pulling down surgical lamp, so that it is directly over chair*): Enough already. You want me to admit that things are grim? Well alright, things are very grim. Mr. Rosenberg is the first client I've had in weeks. *New York* magazine won't even take my ads anymore. I owe them too much money. Make your phone calls now, darling, because I don't know how much longer we'll have a telephone. My few friends, if I can call them that, are all on Medicare or mental disability. (*Unseen by them, Rosenberg stands in the archway wearing Chris' kimono. Chris sits on sofa and nervously fluffs pillows*) I'm at the end of something. I don't know what I'm going to do.

POLLY (*with theatrical tenderness*): I'm here now. (*Notices* ROSENBERG) I've been very naughty keeping you from your client. I think I'll take a nappy. I am emotionally depleted. Don't let me sleep too long, darling. (*She exits through the archway*)

CHRISTOPHER (*extremely tense; retrieving his lab coat from a hook behind front door*): Mr. Rosenberg, you've been very patient. (*Putting on the coat*) I'm going to give you this session free of charge.

ROSENBERG: That's not necessary.

CHRISTOPHER (*lifting top of coffee table, he takes out a pair of rubber gloves*): I may not have a life, but I do have my principles. Please, get in that chair. (*Rosenberg begins to sit in the chair*) On all fours! (*Rosenberg climbs into the chair on his hands and knees. As Chris puts on his rubber gloves, he mutters to himself*) She has some nerve, barging in here . . . telling me what to do.

ROSENBERG: I feel like a collie at the dog show.

CHRISTOPHER (*humorlessly*): Shoulders down. Raise your haunches.

ROSENBERG: Maybe we should do this some other time. You seem a little *fetutzed.*

CHRISTOPHER: I am not *fetutzed.* I am a professional eyeing you with cold objectivity. (*He flips on a light switch on wall just below archway*) Now, we'll find a small area of flesh to experiment on, in case it burns. (*He grabs electrolysis goggles that are hanging just below cabinet*)

ROSENBERG: I think you've got something else on your mind.

CHRISTOPHER (*putting on the goggles and grabbing the electrolysis needle just inside the cabinet*): Mr. Rosenberg, I am a licensed depilatory technician. Now lift that kimono. We will experiment on the buttocks.

(CHRISTOPHER *raises his needle. Mr. Rosenberg looks terrified. Blackout.*)

Scene Two

Several weeks later. Early evening. Polly is standing in the middle of the room wearing a beautiful ball gown. She crosses down left to mirror on wall. The sound of a blow dryer is heard offstage.

POLLY: Christopher, hurry! Flavia and Leonce will be here any minute. Forget the shoes. This gown is so long. No one will even see my feet. (*She picks up a matching shawl from barber chair and puts it on*)

CHRISTOPHER (*offstage*): Be patient. You're going to be ecstatic. I promise you.

POLLY: I shall be extremely cross if I'm late for the Rainbow Room. No, really darling, stop blow drying those pumps. I'm going barefoot. It's a charity ball for the homeless. It'll make a statement. (*To herself*) I wonder if I should wear any rings. No, girl, keep it simple.

CHRISTOPHER (*entering with the matching satin pumps*): Here they are.

POLLY (*dropping shawl back on barber chair*): How'd they come out?

CHRISTOPHER (*showing them to her*): Darling, you'd never know that they were once psychedelic green. (*Putting them on the floor and helping her into them*) They're still slightly damp.

POLLY (*putting them on*): Oh, squishy. (*Crossing left to mirror*) I feel like an extra in "The Poseidon Adventure." What time is it?

CHRISTOPHER: Five to seven.

POLLY: You'd better get going on that seam, bud.

CHRISTOPHER: You treat your staff with such kindness. (*Gets his sewing box from on top of the desk and brings it down to the coffee table*) You know, Polly, no matter what I do, you're still going to strain the seam. (*Taking out a needle and thread*) The dress just doesn't fit. You're too busty. (*He crosses to her left and begins making an adjustment*)

POLLY: Why can't I have the body of a drag queen? I'll never be a perfect four.

CHRISTOPHER: That's because you're a six. I really don't think it's right for us to take apart a borrowed couturier gown.

POLLY: Claudio will be thrilled with the credit. Keep stitching. Ow, you stuck me.

CHRISTOPHER: This might hold. I'm using the same thread the astronauts use.

POLLY: This reminds me of when you use to make costumes for me when we were kids.

CHRISTOPHER: Only my Thanksgiving turkey costume fit you better. (*Finishing the alteration*) There we go.

POLLY (*crossing to coffee table, picking up long satin gloves and putting them on*): Now, if I can only navigate past old Norma's door without her spitting on me.

CHRISTOPHER: She couldn't do that. She's completely paralyzed.

POLLY: Her spitting has the accuracy of a Scud missile. You know she loves you and hates me.

CHRISTOPHER: You're just paranoid because of that silly gift she gave you.

POLLY: A tiny coffin with my wax effigy. (*The intercom buzzer goes off. Polly crosses to it.*) It's Flavia. Wouldn't you know . . . for once she's prompt. (*She answers it*) Sweetness, is that you?

FLAVIA (*on the intercom*): It's Flavia, darling. Hurry, we're double parked.

POLLY (*into intercom*): I'll be right down.

CHRISTOPHER: You really look great. Let me take a picture. Where's the camera?

POLLY: Sweetness, there's no time. You've turned me into a princess. (*Looking through her purse on desk*) Let's see, have I got everything? Lipstick, compact, keys, joints, condoms—where's my lucky rabbit's foot? (*She discovers it on desk, putting it in purse*) Darling, I wish you could come.

CHRISTOPHER: The last thing I'd want to do. Remember every detail and tell me about it in the morning. (*Embracing her*)

POLLY: It shan't be too early. Goodbye darling. (*She opens the door and exits with a flourish*)

CHRISTOPHER (*seeing her earrings on sofa table. Calling off*): Polly, your earrings!

POLLY (*returning and putting the earrings on*): It would serve me right if I forgot the damn things. (*Kisses him on the cheek*) Love you. *Au revoire, mon frère.* (*She strikes a pose in the doorway*) *Je vais à la gloire!* (*Exit*)

(*Christopher sighs, crosses down to coffee table and begins picking up loose threads, fabric and pins off the floor. The intercom buzzer goes off. He picks up sewing stuff, drops it off at desk and runs to the intercom*)

CHRISTOPHER (*into intercom*): Polly, what did you forget?

ROSENBERG (*over intercom*): It's Sy Rosenberg.

CHRISTOPHER: Oh. (*He buzzes him in, turns and notices that Polly has left her matching shawl on barber chair*) She forgot her shawl. (*He runs to the window, opens it and calls down to her*) Polly! Polly! (*She's gone. He crosses to the shawl, picks it up and stands for a minute, transfixed and mesmerized by its elegance. The doorbell rings. Christopher drops the shawl on the window seat and lets Mr. Rosenberg in*) Good evening.

ROSENBERG (*entering*): I saw your sister coming out the front door. She looked very elegant.

CHRISTOPHER (*closing door and crossing to window seat*): We've done nothing for days but get her ready for this big extravaganza and she left her shawl.

ROSENBERG: Oh, yes. Tonight's the charity ball for the M . . .

CHRISTOPHER: Metropolitan Coalition for the Homeless. Everyone's going to be there.

ROSENBERG: Except you and me and the homeless. Do you mind?

CHRISTOPHER: You couldn't drag me to something like that. It sounds hideous. I have this fantasy of what a glamorous ball should be like, something out of Proust or an MGM musical. Somehow, I don't think this one could compare.

ROSENBERG: Maybe not. (*Rosenberg takes off his suit jacket and hands it to Chris*) Damn it, I forgot. I wanted to bring you some real hangers. (*He sits down wearily on the sofa*) I'm forgetting everything these days.

CHRISTOPHER (*hanging jacket on a single metal hanger on a hook in the upstage window*): You look exhausted. I don't mind canceling tonight.

ROSENBERG: No, I look forward to coming here. When Polly's not around, it's extremely restful.

CHRISTOPHER: Restful?

ROSENBERG: It's the conversation, Christopher. If it weren't for that, I think I'd give it up.

CHRISTOPHER: No. Your back and shoulders are almost as smooth as Harlow's. For only six weeks we've made great progress.

ROSENBERG: No one's going to see them.

CHRISTOPHER: You just had a rough day. (*Massages Rosenberg's shoulders*)

ROSENBERG: That feels great. (*Pause*) I still miss Miriam so much. She's more real to me than my own daughter.

CHRISTOPHER: You still haven't called Lenore. You promised me.

ROSENBERG: Those lines of communication are closed.

CHRISTOPHER: What if I called her? I could tell her how much you need her. I could say that you . . .

ROSENBERG: Look Christopher, that would only be a Band-Aid. The fact is she doesn't like me and I know this is a terrible thing for a father to say, but I really don't like her.

CHRISTOPHER (*crossing to barber chair*): She must have some good points. (*Adjusting paper towel behind barber chair*)

ROSENBERG: Lenore inherited her mother's legs and plastic surgeon. Chris, I'm a realistic man. No mumbo jumbo for me. But I want Miriam to haunt me. A tap on the window. Her breath on my cheek. I could live on that.

CHRISTOPHER (*sitting next to Rosenberg*): If you'd like, I could take out my Ouija board. Norma next door gave it to me. Norma once told me that children born at twilight like I was have the power to even see spirits.

ROSENBERG: And have you?

CHRISTOPHER: Hmmm. A few months ago, I'd have put

money down that I saw Hubert Humphrey at the D'Agostino. Should we try to contact Miriam?

ROSENBERG: Let the dead rest. If they could come back, we might not like what they have to say to us.

CHRISTOPHER: I used to wish my mother would haunt me. A couple of years after she fell out the window, I was sure I heard her voice and even caught a glimpse of her in the backyard. I've never seen my father although I've tried. (*Pause*) It's probably a good thing that neither of my parents are floating around here. They'd be pretty disappointed. Polly and I haven't turned out to be exactly any parent's dream. Hey, would you like a drink? I think tonight we could both use a shot of bourbon.

ROSENBERG (*with deep sincerity; taking Christopher by the shoulders*): You know something, kiddo? I think you're just great. (*Christopher is startled by Rosenberg's sincerity. He feels tears welling in his eyes and quickly pulls away*) What's wrong? I've said something?

CHRISTOPHER (*getting up and starting to cry*): Nothing. I'm so embarrassed.

ROSENBERG: Don't be.

CHRISTOPHER (*grabbing a paper towel to wipe his eyes*): This is not like me at all. It's so silly. I suppose I'm just relieved that Polly got off to the Rainbow Room. (*Throwing away paper towel in trash can below electrolysis cabinet*)

ROSENBERG (*getting up*): Christopher, you are going to that ball.

CHRISTOPHER: Huh?

ROSENBERG: You heard me. (*Crossing to desk and picking up phone*) I'm going to make a few phone calls and you are going to that *forcockta* ball.

CHRISTOPHER (*crossing to him and taking the phone out of his hands*): Please don't. I don't want to go. (*Putting phone back on desk*) If I was crying, it's because . . . I don't know . . . you've touched me in some way. Don't do this.

ROSENBERG: Why don't you want to go?

CHRISTOPHER: I'm pathologically shy.

ROSENBERG: You have no trouble talking to me.

CHRISTOPHER: I can only talk to Jewish senior citizens.

ROSENBERG: I hear Kissinger's going to be there.

CHRISTOPHER: I'm serious. Don't make me go.

ROSENBERG: I'm not going to force you to go. I wanted to do a good turn for you.

CHRISTOPHER: Why?

ROSENBERG: Why?

CHRISTOPHER: Why are you doing this? You hardly know me.

ROSENBERG: Do I really need a reason?

CHRISTOPHER: I'd be interested in hearing one.

ROSENBERG: Well, I have the money to indulge myself and I'm in the mood to be extravagant. Does that make you feel better?

CHRISTOPHER: I don't know how I feel.

ROSENBERG: Could it be so extraordinary that I simply like you?

CHRISTOPHER: But you've known me for such a short time.

ROSENBERG: I'm a pretty good judge of character and believe me, you're a character. (*Sitting*) I've never met anyone like you.

CHRISTOPHER: I'm not unique. There are thousands of us living in peculiar circumstances all over the Village.

ROSENBERG: Then I should gather all of you together in the Javits Center. I'd have a helluva time. Look, I get a kick out of you. Must I explain? Chris, sit. (*Chris does so*) You remind me of my father. Yes. Isadore Rosenberg. It's true. You see, my father was a dreamer. He invented the first collapsible suitcase, though he never made a cent from it. He was an immigrant, barely conversant in the English language. Had no business sense. He slaved all of his life at a bench in a factory. But he had a great dignity. It was always "Mr. Rosenberg," never "Izzy." The way we lived. On cold nights, all of us in one bed with our shoes on to keep from freezing, our stomachs rumbling from the eight of us having to share one small pullet for dinner. Hearing the cries of the Polish lady next door giving birth. But despite the hardships, my Papa filled me with such wonderment. He could create magic with a phrase. The stories. How I wish I'd written them down. I'd forgotten how much I needed that magic. You cast the same kind of spell. So let me make a dream come true for you. What do you say?

CHRISTOPHER: It's all so complicated. What would I wear? I don't even have a pair of black shoes.

ROSENBERG: Easily solved. Next anxiety?

CHRISTOPHER: Socks, shirt, tie. Cufflinks. I don't own a pair of cufflinks. Actually, I do have those antique ones with the rhinestone gladioli.

ROSENBERG: We'll get you a pair.

CHRISTOPHER: You really could get me in?

ROSENBERG: One phone call. Judy Cunningham is a pal of mine. It's her charity. Look, I know I can be a steamroller. If you really don't want to go . . .

CHRISTOPHER: I do want to go. I'd love to go.

ROSENBERG: Now he'd love to go. (*Getting up, crossing to phone on desk*) Then, kid, we've gotta get moving.

CHRISTOPHER (*getting up*): What do I do?

ROSENBERG: Get yourself cleaned up. (*Clapping his hands*) Go, go, go!

CHRISTOPHER: I'm going. (*Crossing right and up to archway. He stops*) I can't believe this is happening. (*He exits through the archway*)

ROSENBERG (*picking up the phone and dialing*): Hello, this is Seymour Rosenberg. I'd like to speak to Mrs. Cunningham . . . thank you. (*Pause*) Judy, it's Sy Rosenberg. Dear, forgive me for taking you away from your guests. I'm sure you're all getting ready to leave for the Rainbow Room. I need to ask you a small favor. . . . No, I'm afraid I can't make it, but I have a very dear friend, a young man, a protegé of mine and I'd like very much for him to attend.

(*The lights change. We hear music and the sound of a clock ticking to indicate the passage of time. Rosenberg crosses, is discovered upstage center, making a new phone call*)

ROSENBERG: Hello Morty, Sy Rosenberg. I hope I'm not interrupting your dinner. I'm in a bit of an emergency. I need one of your finest tuxedos. An Armani, something very distinguished and stylish and I need shoes, socks, shirt, cufflinks, the works and I need it delivered in the next twenty minutes. Not for me, for a very dear friend. Well, it's like a fairy tale.

(*Once again, lights, music, ticking. Rosenberg crosses and sits at desk, making a new phone call*)

ROSENBERG: Hello Chickie, Sy Rosenberg. How are ya? Look Chickie, I need a car sent over in a half hour. Not the usual. Something wonderful. Have you got a white Rolls? Perfect. Bill it to me and send the car around to 312 Bank Street, just off of Bleeker. Apartment 2E.

(*Music and ticking sound. The lights get brighter and it's now forty-five minutes later. Christopher enters, transformed. He's wearing an elegant tuxedo and looks like a young prince*)

CHRISTOPHER (*entranced*): How do I look?

ROSENBERG: You're a very handsome young man. I don't want you to say anything. But I would like you to look outside that window.

CHRISTOPHER (*crossing left to window and looking down; astonished*): Is that car supposed to . . .

ROSENBERG: It's a white Rolls. (*Standing*) A little vulgar, but it's fun. It's yours for the night. Enjoy.

CHRISTOPHER: And it won't turn into a pumpkin?

ROSENBERG: It never will. (*Indicating Chris' shoe*) But, don't lose that shoe. It's a rental. (*He crosses to get his coat*)

CHRISTOPHER (*suddenly insecure; crossing to desk, adjusting desk chair and turning off desk lamp. Then, turning off lamp on sofa table*): Mr. Rosenberg, what if I . . . ?

ROSENBERG: You're gonna give your name at the door. You're gonna walk inside, head up, back straight. You're gonna look everyone in the eye and say to yourself, "I have more wit, charm and intelligence than all of you." You're gonna dance, eat and mingle. You've got your keys? You've got cash?

CHRISTOPHER (*very touched*): Yes. I've got everything.

ROSENBERG: You certainly do. Don't waste another minute.

(*Christopher opens the front door. Mr. Rosenberg exits. Christopher turns out light switch on wall just right of door. Overcome with emotion, he stands for a moment in silhouette, then exits. Lights fade.*)

Scene Three

Polly is discovered on the telephone at the desk stage left.

POLLY: Darling, please don't be so upset. I feel awful about
it. Claudio, just calm down. Of course, you know the
dress made a complete sensation. I'm sure the *Times* will
run a photo in the Style section. . . . I know, I know, I
know I promised to return it today, but I just can't. But
darling, you have so many gowns in your collection. Why
must you have this one? Now stop that. You know that I
am the most responsible person in the world. For God's
sake, I take care of my invalid aunt. I know what respon-
sibility and obligation mean. (*Calling off to an imaginary
aunt*) Aunt Rose, do be careful with that walker. Don't
overdo it. Nurse, would you please. . . . Claudio, it's
just madness here. (*The intercom buzzes. Polly crosses to
it, buzzing in Rosenberg downstairs*) No, no. Claudio, you
can't send someone over for the dress, because I'm not
even home. I'm in Paris. Yes, yes, it is a very good con-
nection. I'm afraid I won't be back for at least a week.
Darling, I really must run. Our guide is here. We're taking a private tour of Versailles. You know, all the little
rooms that have been locked up since the revolution. Le
Petit Trianon and everything. (*The doorbell rings. She
opens the door and lets Rosenberg in*) Excuse me, Claudio. (*Polly strategically places down the phone and motions
Rosenberg to be quiet*) *Un moment, monsieur, je suis à la
telephone avec mon couturier en Amerique.* (*Picking up
telephone*) Claudio, you can see I'm just frantic. I'll call
you as soon as I return. Bless you darling. (*She hangs up.
Then to Rosenberg*) Well, if it isn't the Scarsdale fairy
godfather.

ROSENBERG: Good afternoon, Polly.

POLLY: Your friend Cinderella is visiting the old crone next door and will be home shortly. May I get you some coffee? We're running a bit late today.

ROSENBERG: No, thank you. I'll just get changed. (*He exits through the archway. From off*) Were you surprised to see your brother at the Rainbow Room?

POLLY: Surprised is hardly the word. Contrary to rumor, I am not the wicked stepsister. I was thrilled to see Chris all dolled up and so downright vivacious. I can't thank you enough for doing this.

ROSENBERG: Did you have a splendid time?

POLLY: I don't know if I'd say "splendid." It certainly was fraught with drama. It was all so silly, really. This, um, gentleman friend of mine lent me some pieces of his wife's jewelry for the evening. Well, I guess he hadn't told her and didn't realize she'd be there last night. Naturally, she recognized the jewelry and it all got rather ugly. Food flying. But, the good news is that the stain on the dress will come out.

ROSENBERG (*re-entering through archway*): I'm sure it'll all be forgotten by tomorrow.

CHRISTOPHER (*entering through the door*): Mr. Rosenberg, I hope I haven't kept you waiting. Please, have a seat. I'll be right with you. (*Rosenberg sits in the barber chair. Christopher grabs his lab coat and puts it on*) I was next door telling Norma all about last night. You should see her, Polly. I actually got her to put her dentures in. I swear she looks exactly like Agnes Moorehead. (*He opens the electrolysis cabinet behind the barber chair*) We really should get started. I'm not in a rush, but I met someone last night and he's coming over in a few hours.

POLLY (*overjoyed*): You met your prince.

CHRISTOPHER: I don't know about that. He's a publicist. (*Opening the coffee table to remove an instrument and rubber gloves*) He's quite young, but he's worked with everyone from Lainie Kazan to serial killers.

POLLY (*suggesting that there might've been more to Christopher's encounter*): Mmm hmm?

CHRISTOPHER: Don't get excited, Polly. It was just a romantic night. I'm not getting married.

ROSENBERG (*sincerely surprised*): You're a . . . homosexual?

POLLY (*incredulously acid*): Oh no.

ROSENBERG (*embarrassed*): Not that it's an issue. Not at all. I'm a liberal. I . . . I . . . It never occurred to me. There's nothing effeminate about you.

POLLY (*confused*): We are talking about *my* brother?

CHRISTOPHER (*irritated*): Yes, Polly.

ROSENBERG (*fumbling*): Well, there's nothing to discuss. You're a gay. Big deal. Everyone has a right to. . . . Today, it's the "in" thing. *Angels in America*. Far be for me to. . . . So, um, Chris, your new friend—is he handsome?

CHRISTOPHER (*amused*): Uh huh.

POLLY: Is he rich?

CHRISTOPHER: I don't think so.

ROSENBERG: Is he Jewish?

CHRISTOPHER: Yes. (*He turns on the electrolysis machine*) His name is Walter Zuckerman. We hit it off and he's coming over later. That's really all there is to it.

ROSENBERG (*pleased*): What a night you must have had.

CHRISTOPHER: It was perhaps the greatest night of my life. Here I was actually thinking of going back to Albuquerque, but now I never want to leave this warm, friendly, quaint little city.

ROSENBERG: Did you meet Judy Cunningham?

CHRISTOPHER: Oh yes. She found me almost the minute I arrived and she introduced me to everyone. It was like I was wearing an enchanted tuxedo. Words just tumbled out of my mouth. (*To Polly*) Darling, you've never seen such poise outside of a Constance Bennett picture. I spoke with Mario Buatta and Dina Merrill and, let's see, um, Spaulding Grey and Betty Comden—she was awfully nice—and Orson Bean. (*He puts on the rubber gloves*)

POLLY: My word.

ROSENBERG: You see, you can relate to people. Next time, it'll be even easier.

CHRISTOPHER: I'm not sure I can do it without the tuxedo. By the way, everything is packed and ready to go back.

ROSENBERG: It's paid for. It's yours to keep.

CHRISTOPHER: You can't do that. It's too much.

(*Rosenberg motions him to say no more*)

POLLY: Isn't that marvelous. I don't suppose the Rolls is . . .

ROSENBERG: That went back.

(*Christopher removes a cotton ball and rubbing alcohol from the cabinet and begins to prep* ROSENBERG'*s neck and shoulders*)

POLLY (*stumbling to get out of the awkward situation*): Oh, yes . . . I'm sure. I was just wondering. . . . (*Sighs*) Well, darling, if you're Cinderella, I must be Sleeping Beauty. Last night had a bit too much mad frenzy for me. Wake me up before the century turns. (*Exiting through the archway*)

ROSENBERG: My, but it's close in here. Maybe you could turn on the air conditioner.

CHRISTOPHER: It is awfully fierce.

ROSENBERG: I hope you have that thing serviced yearly. You don't want it to die on you during the hottest day of the summer.

(*Christopher turns on the old unit which rumbles to a start. The lights in the room dim. The air conditioner has created a*

power surge, altering the electrical output in the room. Chris-
topher returns to his work)

ROSENBERG: This young man who's coming over. You really
like him?

CHRISTOPHER: Sure, but it's just a first impression.

ROSENBERG: I'm a believer in first impressions. You two
have similar interests?

CHRISTOPHER: Oh yes. He loves old movies. Especially
Women's Prison starring Ida Lupino. (*He dons the elec-*
trolysis goggles) I always used to fantasize that she was
my mother. (*Christopher removes the electrically charged*
electrolysis needle from the cabinet and begins to go to
work. He manipulates a foot pedal at the base of the chair
which operates the pen. We hear the needle buzz twice. On
the second buzz, every major lighting fixture in the room
goes on and off individually. There is obviously something
wrong with the electricity. Christopher says matter-of-factly)
The wiring in this building is so decrepit. You can't have
too many appliances on at the same time. For instance, I
can't simultaneously blow dry my hair, use a power tool
and make toast. I'm afraid I'm going to have to turn off
the air conditioner. (*He grabs a paper towel from below*
the cabinet to protect his sterile gloves, crosses to the air
conditioner and turns it off) The landlord keeps promis-
ing to rewire this building. (*He crosses down to the win-*
dow and opens it) Sometimes if I open this window, I get
a good breeze from the river. Let's get cracking. (*Chris-*
topher returns to Rosenberg, picks up the needle and starts
to work again. We hear another buzz. Rosenberg flinches)
I'm so sorry. Did you get a shock? (*Suddenly Rosenberg*
gasps, has a heart seizure and collapses. He is motionless
and quite dead. Christopher is oblivious to Rosenberg as he

stares at the needle to figure out the problem) That's never happened before. (*He looks down and thinks that Rosenberg is pulling a prank*) Mr. Rosenberg. Mr. Rosenberg? C'mon. (*Suddenly aware that something terrible has happened, he begins to gently slap Rosenberg on the face*) Mr. Rosenberg? Are you alright? Mr. Rosenberg? Polly!

(*In hysterics, Christopher exits through the archway. The following dialogue is heard from offstage*)

CHRISTOPHER: Polly! Come here quick!

POLLY: What is it?

CHRISTOPHER: It's Mr. Rosenberg. Something happened to him. He's unconscious. The electric current must have been too strong. He's had some sort of seizure. (*The two bolt through the archway, Polly leading the way. She picks up Rosenberg's wrist, trying to detect a pulse. Then, she leans over to listen to his heart. Finally, she waves her hand in front of his face to detect breathing. Christopher paces through the whole process*) Is he alright? Of course he's alright.

POLLY (*dropping Rosenberg's arm in repulsion*): He's dead.

CHRISTOPHER (*pushing her away and grabbing Rosenberg*): No, he's not! Wake up. Wake up!

POLLY: His heart isn't beating at all.

CHRISTOPHER: Don't say that. (*Near tears and feverishly slapping Rosenberg*) Mr. Rosenberg, please, wake up!

POLLY: Chris, stop it! He's dead. This is no time for hysterics.

CHRISTOPHER (*on the verge of hysteria*): Polly, you don't
seem to understand. I have executed another Rosenberg! I am a murderer!

POLLY: He was an old man. He never looked well. He most
likely had a heart attack.

CHRISTOPHER (*realizing his loss, kneeling beside Rosenberg*): He can't be gone. I couldn't even say goodbye. I
can't even say goodbye.

POLLY: You do have malpractice insurance, don't you?

CHRISTOPHER: I never got around to it. Oh, I don't care. I
accept my punishment.

POLLY: There's only one thing for us to do.

CHRISTOPHER: What's that?

POLLY: Ditch the body. If we can squeeze him through the
bathroom window, he'd fall into the air shaft. We'll need
alibis and good ones. I don't suppose your friend Orson
Bean would take us in? (*The intercom buzzes. Polly answers it*) Hello? Who's there?

WALTER (*on intercom*): Walter Zuckerman. Is Chris there?

CHRISTOPHER: Oh my God.

POLLY (*into intercom*): I'm sorry. My brother just stepped
out.

CHRISTOPHER (*rushing to the intercom, pushing Polly out of
the way*): Walter, you're rather early.

Charles Busch as Christopher *(right)* with Nell Campbell as Polly *(center)* and Stephen Pearlman as Mr. Rosenberg.

All photos of the 1994 Primary Stages production by Andrew Leynse.

Charles Busch as Christopher *(behind)* with Nell Campbell as Polly *(right)* and Stephen Pearlman as Mr. Rosenberg.

Charles Busch as Christopher *(left)* with Jennifer Kato as Wanda Wang *(center)* and Julie Halston as Lenore Rosenberg.

(From left to right) Nell Campbell as Polly, Jennifer Kato as Wanda Wang,
Matthew Arkin as Walter, Charles Busch as Christopher
and Julie Halston as Lenore.

WALTER (*on intercom*): No. We said three.

CHRISTOPHER: I thought it was four. I may need a few . . .

WALTER (*on intercom*): I'm having trouble understanding you. There's static.

CHRISTOPHER: This may not be the best time . . .

WALTER (*on intercom*): Hello? Hello? Someone's opening the door downstairs. I'll come up.

CHRISTOPHER: Oh my God.

POLLY: Ditch the body!

CHRISTOPHER: No, no. We won't do that. I need time. Help me bring him over to the sofa. We'll lie him down there and cover him with throws and pillows. (*He crosses down to clear the coffee table*) I'll keep Walter distracted. We won't even let him into the apartment. Help me move him.

POLLY: He's a big man and my back's never recovered from that last *Godspell.*

CHRISTOPHER: We've got to hurry. We need to clear all the pillows and throws off the sofa. (*In a mad frenzy, they pull everything off the sofa and then cross to either side of the body. The doorbell rings*) Is that you, Walter?

WALTER (*through the door*): It's me.

CHRISTOPHER: I'll be right there. (*To Polly*) Now, let's flip him over gently like a crepe. (*Beginning to lift the body*) Let's lift him up gingerly. Gingerly. (*They walk the body to the center of the sofa. All three fall backwards onto the sofa*) You take his legs. I'll get his head. (*They position the body across the sofa. Rosenberg's knees are bent. Polly pushes down on them with one lunge and the body is perfectly placed. Christopher starts draping the body with a velvet Victorian throw*) Now, let's drape everything over him for a nice, casual effect. (*Christopher starts heaving pillows at Polly. The two place colorful pillows all around and over the corpse to disguise its contours*) Darling, that red one would look ever so much prettier beside the puce.

POLLY: This is silly.

WALTER (*offstage*): Chris! Hello!

(*Christopher dashes to the door, with Polly at his heels. Christopher realizes he is still wearing the lab coat. He frantically takes it off. Polly helps and hangs it up. Chris straightens himself and opens the door*)

CHRISTOPHER: Here I am.

(*Walter is a good-looking guy in his thirties. Somewhat neurotic, it doesn't interfere with his natural charm*)

WALTER: I thought you forgot about me.

CHRISTOPHER: I certainly did not. (*He ushers Walter in and closes the door*) Walter, this is my sister, Polly.

POLLY: Hello, Walter.

WALTER: I have a feeling I caught you off-guard.

CHRISTOPHER: I suppose you have. I . . . I . . . I was nude.

POLLY: So was I. We're nudists.

CHRISTOPHER (*regretting that line*): Experimenting with it. It was our first time. Doubt we'll ever do it again. It's such a beautiful day. Polly, we're going for a walk.

WALTER: Must we? (*He crosses to the front of the sofa*) It's so hot. On the radio, they said a schnauzer exploded on Third Avenue. Can we sit down?

(*Christopher crosses down and intercepts Walter's attempt to sit on the sofa, ushering him to a hideous, metal, straightback chair with a tiny triangular seat. It's more sculpture than chair*)

CHRISTOPHER: Of course. Why don't you sit over here. It's so much nicer.

(*Walter sits with great effort*)

WALTER (*sincerely*): Gee, I thought this was an ashtray.

CHRISTOPHER: It's based on a sculpture by Giacometti.

(*Christopher and Polly, with nowhere else to sit, kneel just right of Walter*)

WALTER: Must you kneel? I feel like Hans Christian Andersen.

CHRISTOPHER: Polly, why don't we relax on the sofa?

(Polly and Christopher carefully sit on the sofa, but oddly perched on the farthest edge)

WALTER: You don't look very relaxed. You look in agony. You know, the most fascinating thing happened . . .

POLLY *(rising abruptly)*: I really must go. *(She crosses to the door and opens it)*

CHRISTOPHER: I don't want to chase you out.

POLLY: You're not at all. I'll be right back.

CHRISTOPHER: But you've got nothing on underneath that robe.

POLLY: So true. I suppose I'll try this nudist thing out on Mrs. Abbotelli on the front stoop. Lovely meeting you, Walter. Bye. *(She exits)*

WALTER: You did want to get together today?

CHRISTOPHER: Oh yes.

WALTER: For a minute there, I wasn't sure. Since last night, I've thought a lot about you.

CHRISTOPHER: Same here.

WALTER: It's the strangest thing. I feel like I've known you for, I don't know, forever. It's like we can dispense with all the preliminaries of friendship and just be, you know, for real.

CHRISTOPHER: How do you want to be real?

WALTER: Ask important questions. Have you ever been in love?

CHRISTOPHER: No.

WALTER: Have you ever been in therapy?

CHRISTOPHER: No.

WALTER: I guess these are dumb questions. Do you have a terrible fear of death?

CHRISTOPHER (*sprawling across the corpse, appearing more casual*) Not as much as I thought. You get sort of used to it. What do you think about death? I mean *really* think about it?

WALTER (*crossing around couch and then to archway, taking in the room*): One of my first jobs when I came to New York was with The *Daily News*. I assisted the photographer who shot murder victims. After awhile, nothing shocks you.

CHRISTOPHER (*encouraged*): Walter, I should explain something to you. Remember I told you I perform electrolysis on people? Well, I have this client, a wonderful man. He sent me to the ball last night just like . . .

WALTER (*coming down to sofa*): The girl with the glass shoe. That was his Rolls Royce?

CHRISTOPHER: He paid for it. I have a confession to make.

WALTER: He's your sugar daddy? That's cool. I'm not judgmental. My cousin Francine is a professional dominatrix.

CHRISTOPHER: . . . Skip it.

WALTER: Listen, I can't believe I told you all about my rotten childhood and therapy.

CHRISTOPHER (*rising*): No, I find your neuroses absolutely fascinating. I really do.

WALTER: You don't think I'm just a spoiled, suburban Jew?

CHRISTOPHER: No. Please. I mean, that whole thing about your brother making you believe you were Filipino. That's hardly standard-issue suburban angst.

WALTER: Is that couch just for display, or can we actually recline on it?

CHRISTOPHER (*sitting nervously and fluffing pillows*): A neighbor's cat shed all over the pillows. If you have any allergies at all . . .

WALTER (*sitting on sofa arm*): I'm that rarity. A neurotic without allergies. (*He sits next to Chris and nuzzles his neck*)

(*Throughout the next speech, Walter seduces Christopher, kissing his neck and finally pulling his left arm up and kissing it from top to bottom*)

CHRISTOPHER (*guilt-ridden*): Walter, I'd think twice about seducing me. My mother, who had a very *slight* drinking problem, fell out of her window while writing a poem. And my father, my father had his head bitten off while performing a Punch and Judy Show at the zoo. I am dogged by bad luck.

WALTER: I love it. Tell me more.

(*Walter throws Chris' left arm around his neck and tackles him directly back on the sofa. The force of the tackle dislodges Rosenberg's arm from underneath the throw and pillows*)

CHRISTOPHER: Walter, please.

(*Christopher discovers Rosenberg's arm and is near hysteria. With Walter on top of him, Chris pulls his body left to try to cover the hand. Unsuccessful, he tries to stuff the hand underneath him. Walter's head comes up. In a panic, Chris stuffs his own left arm underneath himself, while grabbing Rosenberg's hand with his right hand, making it seem as if Rosenberg's hand is his own*)

WALTER: Am I too heavy on you?

CHRISTOPHER: No.

(*Walter kisses down Chris' right arm to his hand and then on to kissing the dead hand. Christopher is horrified*)

WALTER (*nestling his head on Christopher's chest*): Your hand is cold.

CHRISTOPHER: And prematurely aged. (*Walter continues his advances with fervor*) Walter, stop. Stop!

(*Christopher pushes Walter off him and pulls the throw and pillow away to reveal Rosenberg's face. Walter screams in wild hysteria. He runs. Chris follows*)

WALTER: Who is this man?

CHRISTOPHER: Seymour Rosenberg.

WALTER: You killed him?

CHRISTOPHER: Possibly. If I did cause his death, it wasn't intentional. I was performing electrolysis on him and he died from a sudden heart seizure.

WALTER: I kissed his dead hand.

CHRISTOPHER: Yes, but he was a great man. You would have liked him and he was so happy that I was dating a Jewish boy.

WALTER (*eyeing the telephone on the desk*): We must call the police. This man needs to be buried. You weren't planning on keeping him here, were you?

CHRISTOPHER: Walter, I'm not a ghoul. I'm just an unlucky electrologist with a sense of whimsy.

WALTER: I'll call the police if you'd like.

CHRISTOPHER: Thank you and thank you for sticking around. You really didn't have to. As a matter of fact, maybe you should leave. I've never killed anyone before, but for some reason, it seems indicative of my lifestyle. (*Looking for Walter's coat*) You shouldn't get involved. You didn't bring a jacket or anything, did you?

WALTER (*following Chris*): What? Are you kicking me out?

CHRISTOPHER: I'm making it easy for you.

WALTER: What if I don't want to go?

CHRISTOPHER: Walter, look at me. Look at the way I live. It's not romantic. It's pathetic. This mess. Dust everywhere. Woodwork half stripped. Fresh cadaver.

WALTER: So?

CHRISTOPHER (*starting to open door*): It was wonderful meeting you, Walter.

WALTER (*spinning Chris around and holding him by the shoulders*): I don't think you understand where I'm coming from. I'm attracted to you both physically and morbidly.

CHRISTOPHER: What?

WALTER: It's situations like this that made me want to move to New York. I grew up in the San Fernando Valley, for chrissakes. It's nothing but malls, suntan lotion and car washes. I crave darkness. You are dark. (*Christopher is oddly intrigued by Walter's monologue*) Lonely rooms at midnight, insane fantasies, the grotesque. You embody all this. I wanted to live on the edge and experience heightened emotions. This is our first date. (*Looking down at the dead body*) Where can we go from here?

CHRISTOPHER: I would like to kiss you. Just once before the police arrive.

WALTER: Before the eyes of a dead man?

CHRISTOPHER: Yes, I think he would approve.

WALTER (*backing away from Christopher*): Please, Chris, not here. You're going too far.

CHRISTOPHER (*like a High Priestess; almost stalking Walter*): Kiss me.

WALTER (*backing up toward archway*): I'm a very defiant person. I really am. I'd kiss you anywhere else. I mean it. At an army induction center, at Temple Emanuel, at a Knicks game.

CHRISTOPHER (*advancing on him*): Now.

WALTER (*in terror, disappearing through archway*): Noooo!

(*In a very melodramatic style, Christopher parts the beaded curtain at the archway. A very loud organ chord is heard. Blackout.*)

Scene Four

One month later. Midafternoon. Walter is discovered straightening up the room, feather duster in hand. He restores the coffee table and arranges pillows back onto the sofa. Polly enters through the archway wearing a short skirt and camisole, blouse in hand. Walter begins dusting everything in sight.

POLLY (*pulling out the ironing board that is hidden Murphy Bed-style behind a mirror*): This is utterly ridiculous. How is it possible that I can perfectly scan a Shakespearean text, yet I am unable to iron a simple blouse? I do so want to make a good impression on Mr. Rosenberg's daughter. I've ironed this seven times and look at it. As wrinkled as an elderly scrotum.

WALTER: Polly, all morning I've watched you torture that helpless garment. I cannot tell you how much I've

wanted to rip that goddamned iron out of your hands
and iron that thing properly.

POLLY: Darling, why on earth haven't you?

WALTER: I don't want to appear controlling. It's an issue
I'm working on in my therapy.

POLLY: I won't tell a soul. Please, be my guest.

WALTER (*dropping the feather duster on the sofa*): Thank
you. (*He grabs the blouse and pushes Polly center. He
takes the plugged iron from the desk behind him and begins
to iron expertly. Polly sits on the sofa table*) It's the taking
over part. I can feel myself turning into my mother. It's
awful. I distrust every generous act. By being helpful, am
I really saying, "Give me that thing. You can't do anything right, you little schmeggegie. I'm in control around
here. Me! Me!" It's my mother, Evelyn Zuckerman,
speaking. Suddenly, I'm wearing a metaphorical beige
pantsuit.

POLLY: I had no idea. Well, I appreciate the gesture, no
matter what the motive. I think you're the most perfectly
divine brother-in-law.

WALTER: Shhh. I wouldn't use that term in front of you-
know-who.

POLLY: You-know-who who's dressing in the next room?
Oh, a little tension in the house of bliss?

WALTER: I wish there were. Chris and I have been seeing
each other for a month now and I don't even know if he
likes me. I hope he does. I have this great need to create
a home with someone that's stable and loving and nur-

turing. I know that alienates a lot of people. I'd love to be owned, manipulated and even exploited. It all sounds great. (*The ironing is finished*)

POLLY (*rising and taking blouse from Walter*): He just doesn't articulate things. Chris and I are almost like twins. I know he's mad about you. (*She puts on blouse at the mirror*)

WALTER (*putting away the iron*): Can't he just say, "I love you"?

POLLY: Forget that. We don't say that sort of thing. We come from generations of cold, brittle sophisticates.

(*Christopher enters wearing chinos, matching vest, tie and a madras sports jacket that is several sizes too small. He carries a tray of cheese and crackers. Walter crosses down, puts the ironing board away*)

CHRISTOPHER: Jarlsberg and saltines, perfect.

POLLY: Christopher, are you posing as a lesbian?

CHRISTOPHER (*placing the tray on the coffee table*): How astute of you, Polly. I wish to project cool, no-nonsense strength. This is, after all, my first meeting with the daughter of the man I killed.

WALTER: Stop that. You were never charged with anything. Remember, I was there. I filled out the forms with you. I spoke with the police. I showed them the fuse box. I took over. I was controlling every minute of it!

(*The intercom buzzes*)

POLLY: That must be the Stupacks.

CHRISTOPHER (*answering the intercom*): Hello?

LENORE (*on intercom*): Lenore Stupack.

CHRISTOPHER (*into intercom*): We're on the second floor. (*To Polly*) Polly, please don't threaten the Stupacks with your unbridled sexuality.

POLLY: This outfit couldn't be more conservative.

WALTER: Look, the poor woman is probably still in deep mourning. Both of you, be very sensitive and respectful. She's contacted you because she obviously feels some sort of bond. . . . (*eyeing Polly's outfit*) Polly, fix your blouse.

CHRISTOPHER: I think the blouse you had on yesterday was . . .

WALTER: Chris, check your fly. And the most important thing is to . . . (*the doorbell rings. Chris goes to answer the door*) Answer the door.

(*Christopher opens the door. Lenore Rosenberg Stupack is a very stylish and very fierce suburban matron in her early forties. She speaks in a somewhat nasal New York accent, overlaid with pretension*)

CHRISTOPHER: Hello, I'm Christopher. Please come in. (*She does so and upon Chris' introductions, makes her way to sofa*) This is my sister Polly and this is Walter Zuckerman.

WALTER: Good to meet you.

POLLY: So delighted. I've heard so much about you from your wonderful father. Please, sit down. Where is Mr. Stupack?

LENORE: For a half hour he's been trying to find a parking place for the LeSabre. I really can't stay very long.

CHRISTOPHER: I thought we could go for lunch. There are so many charming . . .

LENORE (*abruptly*): We brunched before we came into the city. (*She sits*)

(*Perplexed by Lenore's coldness and abruptness, Christopher, taking in the scene, crosses to the barber chair*)

WALTER: Did your father speak to you of his friendship with Christopher?

LENORE: No. Never. Not a word was ever uttered. This is all such a surprise to me. (*To Chris*) I understand you were performing electrolysis on him?

CHRISTOPHER (*sitting in barber chair*): Yes. He started out as my client, but we became close friends.

LENORE (*seemingly annoyed*): I was going to wait until my husband got here, but he could take until the millennium to find a parking spot in this neighborhood. Let me get to the point.

CHRISTOPHER: Please.

LENORE: Shortly before my father passed on, he made a rather startling change in his will. It's stated that half of his estate, adding up to ten million dollars after taxes, should go to this completely unknown person, a person with no blood ties and no previous history. Ten million dollars that, by all rights, should go to his only child, Lenore Marjorie Rosenberg Stupack.

CHRISTOPHER (*sincerely*): How awful. Who is this strange person and what mysterious hold did he have over Mr. Rosenberg?

WALTER: Chris . . .

CHRISTOPHER: So, you've come to me to find out who this hateful person is.

WALTER (*crossing to Chris*): They know who it is.

CHRISTOPHER: Well, who is it? Is it someone I know?

LENORE (*losing all poise; getting up*): It's you!

POLLY (*gasping and reaching across sofa to Christopher*): Ah . . . ahh . . . ahhhh!!

CHRISTOPHER: Me? I'm the . . . I've inherited ten mil . . . ten million dollars. To think that Mr. Rosenberg wanted to protect me. That he cared so much about me. I can't believe it.

POLLY (*sobbing; kneeling at Chris' feet*): Chris, all the terrible things that have happened to us all our lives have paid off. (*Rising*) My brother is such a good person, in some ways a saint. The good deeds he does for people, the sick, the lame.

CHRISTOPHER (*rising and crossing down center*): We won't be selfish. We'll make great gifts to charity. We'll cure AIDS. We'll save the American Ballet Theatre.

LENORE: Perhaps I haven't made myself clear . . .

CHRISTOPHER (*crossing to Lenore*): Let me ask you just one question. Did you get the other half of the estate?

LENORE: Well, yes, of course, but . . .

CHRISTOPHER: Oh, I'm so relieved. I know you and your father had your problems, but he'd never be so cruel as to. . . . So, at least you're taken care of. It would mean a lot to me if we could embrace. I think your father would want that. (*He reaches out to her*)

LENORE (*repulsed*): What? (*Christopher has fully embraced her. She struggles and throws him back to the sofa*) Get off me! What is this? A mind game? Is this how you bamboozled my father? Well, you may have swindled a sick old man, but I've got news for you. My husband, Leonard, is an attorney with Mossberg, Lieberman, Melnick, Fein and Glick. They'll fucking destroy you!

CHRISTOPHER (*sitting on sofa*): Oh, dear.

LENORE: We find the contents of my father's alleged last will and testament to be completely and utterly unacceptable.

CHRISTOPHER: You want me to give some of it back?

LENORE: You will give all of it back! (*Calming down, picking up a valise she had placed on the coffee table and crossing to the desk*) I'd like to have waited for my husband, but in this neighborhood, he's probably been mugged and/or verbally abused. (*Opening valise and pulling out an official looking document and pen*) At any rate, I've got a document here for you to peruse and sign. It's a renunciation waiver. (*She hands it and a pen to Christopher*) Sign beside the red arrows.

WALTER: A renunciation waiver? That means that he renounces all claim to his inheritance.

LENORE: That is correct.

POLLY: Chris, you don't have to sign anything.

CHRISTOPHER (*reading*): "I renounce all claim to . . ."

(*An otherworldly sound is heard. The ghost of Rosenberg appears. He looks much the same as he did in life, perhaps a bit more pale, but still in the same three-piece suit*)

ROSENBERG: Christopher, put down that pen.

(*Christopher turns and sees Rosenberg. He turns back to us in horror. Beyond shock, a silent scream overtakes him. He crawls down from the sofa to behind Polly and Walter*)

POLLY (*to* LENORE): Look what you've done. My brother is a very fragile creature.

CHRISTOPHER (*pointing to Rosenberg*): Polly, what do you see over there?

POLLY (*unable to see the ghost, she sees a portrait on the wall behind him*): Just that depressing portrait you painted of me with my old nose.

LENORE (*taking a cellular phone from the valise and crossing to the window*): This entire affair is extremely painful for me.

CHRISTOPHER: Polly, squint your eyes and try to . . .

ROSENBERG: How the hell did I get here? Suddenly there was a whoosh and down the hatch I went.

CHRISTOPHER: Can anyone else . . .

WALTER: What?

ROSENBERG (*trying to communicate with others*): Lenore! Polly! Hello? (*Crossing to Chris*) I think only you have the pleasure of my company.

CHRISTOPHER: Walter, do you think a mind can really snap?

WALTER: Don't worry. We're going to work this out.

ROSENBERG: I'm glad to see it's working out with your friend.

CHRISTOPHER: Oh, Walter is very . . .

WALTER: Chris, I'm right here.

ROSENBERG: Don't answer me. They'll think you're meshuga. (*Urging Chris to sit on sofa. Sitting himself. Polly and Walter, concerned about Chris, confer about his mental state*) Chris, I don't know what I'm doing here, but I do know that I want you to have that money. I think you could do great things with ten million bucks for yourself and others. So, don't you dare sign that waiver.

LENORE (*replacing the cellular phone*): I'm sure we can all part as friends.

ROSENBERG: That money is yours. Say it.

CHRISTOPHER (*tentatively*): This money is mine?

POLLY (*surprised*): Chris!

CHRISTOPHER (*stronger*): This money's mine. (*Convinced*) This money's mine. He wants me to have it.

LENORE: This means war.

ROSENBERG: Rip it up. That'll really frost her.

CHRISTOPHER (*picking up the document and crossing to Lenore*): And furthermore . . . (*ripping up the paper*) this is what you can do with this document, or should I rip it up smaller so you can use it by the sheet?

ROSENBERG: I like that.

LENORE: How dare you! How dare you!

CHRISTOPHER: Lenore, your father and I had a very special communication between us. He's still so vivid to me that I'm seeing visions of him like Our Lady Of Fatima.

ROSENBERG: I hadn't thought of myself that way.

CHRISTOPHER: Stop it! I can't take it anymore!

LENORE: You're buckling under 'cause you know you're a fraud. You never knew my father and do you know how I

know you never knew him? Because my father was not a
kind man.

CHRISTOPHER: He was very kind to me.

LENORE: My father was a controlling, tightfisted man of
business. All my life he showered me with presents: the
prettiest pink party dresses, my own pony, a speed boat
called "The Lenore." But in the department store of his
heart, there was no merchandise. The floor was empty.
Nothing I could do was right. He didn't approve of my
bas mitzvah performance, nor my choice of college so-
rority. Not even my choice of husband. Not one of my
houses, not a one. Not a one of my houses would he
approve of. All I wanted was a simple, "Lenore, the
house, the grounds . . . beautiful. Honey, yah done
good." But no. You know what I got? "The trellis needs
pruning." The trellis needs pruning? That was my father.
The man was ice. I could've been dying of cancer and
he'd say, "The trellis needs pruning." My father . . .
my father. I was an asthmatic child. Twice, I nearly died.
Was my father at my bedside? No. Where was the man?
On the phone, talking to his broker. Twenty-seven years
of intensive psychotherapy, acupuncture, scalding baths
and the efforts of a German woman in Jersey City who
sticks chopsticks up my nose—twenty-seven years of torture has taught me that my asthma was psychosomati-
cally induced! My father was literally strangling the
breath from my body! I had to scream at the gestalt
therapist, "Daddy, let me breathe! Let me breathe!"
And you have the temerity to imply that I didn't know
my father?

ROSENBERG (*at a loss*): The trellis needed pruning.

LENORE: I knew my father damned well!

ROSENBERG (*sincerely*): I know I've made some terrible mistakes, but I loved that child.

LENORE: I am owed those monies.

WALTER: I think you should talk to our lawyer . . . when we get one.

LENORE: I will contest this will to the bloody end. We were prepared to make you a settlement of ten thousand dollars, oh yes. But now, you know how much you'll get? Bupkis. My husband works very closely with the District Attorney. Leonard will give him a call and the D.A. will reopen this case. We always suspected there was something fishy going on around here.

WALTER: The police cleared Chris of all charges.

LENORE: Believe me, the D.A. won't find it hard to convince a grand jury to indict the electrologist here of murder.

CHRISTOPHER: Murder?

ROSENBERG: Take the gamble.

CHRISTOPHER: The gamble.

LENORE (*backing Chris to window seat*): The lies you must have fed him. And then, the cold, calculating act of murder. Electrocution? You fried my father!

POLLY: You have said quite enough, Mrs. Stupack. You don't know how many times I heard my brother trying to convince your father that you weren't a selfish, money-hungry bitch!

CHRISTOPHER: Polly, don't do this.

POLLY: Someone has to tell her. My brother even had the ridiculously sentimental notion of trying to bring you and your father back together again.

LENORE: Don't you talk to me. I know all about you. (*Crossing to Polly*) Judy Cunningham told me what a whore you are. She told me Sylvia Tannenbaum's son literally tossed your clothes out the window to get rid of you. I know you screwed Rita Landman's husband, Murray, in the men's room of Tavern On The Green.

(*Polly slaps her across the face. Lenore is stunned*)

ROSENBERG (*sadly*): My foolish girl.

LENORE: You are looking at an assault charge. (*Wildly*) Where is my FUCKING HUSBAND? You and your brother are going to need a good lawyer.

WALTER (*crossing to door*): Mrs. Stupack, this has gone on far too long. I think you should leave.

LENORE: With pleasure, fag! (*Crossing to pick up her valise on the desk, she stops. To Christopher*) Murderer! (*Back to door, she stops. To Polly*) Whore! (*She exits. Walter closes the door*)

POLLY: No matter how much you tip the attendant, they always tell. (*She collapses on sofa in tears*)

ROSENBERG: I am deeply ashamed of the fruit of my loins. Chris, everything's going to work out.

CHRISTOPHER: Please, go away. Go away? You're not even here. You're a very bad migraine. (*Sits in barber chair*)

POLLY: Oh, thanks. Kick me while I'm down, why don't you.

WALTER: Stop this, both of you. I've got an idea. We're going to fight this with the best weapon I have. Publicity.

POLLY (*perking up*): Publicity?

WALTER: The Stupacks could kill us in court. We need a public outcry. (*Kneeling by Chris*) We need to humiliate them with their own greed. I can create this in the media. This is a great story and I could get you a ton of publicity. That's my job.

ROSENBERG (*excitedly getting up*): This guy's on the ball. Listen to him.

POLLY: Talk shows. We'd be great on talk shows.

ROSENBERG: This is terrific!

CHRISTOPHER: I couldn't do that. I was too shy to raise my hand in class. I'm even pee shy.

WALTER: I promise you, Chris, you won't have to pee on *Geraldo*.

ROSENBERG: Kid, you gotta stay in the game.

CHRISTOPHER: Can't any of you see that there's a ghost in this room? (*Walter turns away in disgust*)

POLLY (*angered*): Chris, I swear. If you bring up Mommy and Daddy one more time. . . . (*Rising*) Bury the dead. Get on with your life. Think of that goddamned amaryllis and bloom, Christopher, bloom!

CHRISTOPHER (*getting up and crossing to couch*): No talk shows. I'll tell you that right now. No talk shows.

POLLY: I'll teach you everything I know about being fabulous.

WALTER: You're perfect the way you are. The entire country's going to have a love affair with you.

CHRISTOPHER: That sounds fatiguing.

(*The three sit, simultaneously, on the couch. Polly and Walter plan their strategy while Christopher protests. Rosenberg, not about to be left out, sits perched on the back right of the sofa, offering his advice. Music builds, as the lights fade. End of Act One.*)

ACT
TWO

ACT TWO

Scene One

Christopher's apartment, two days later. Christopher enters through the front door, carrying a large laundry basket and keys. Mr. Rosenberg follows him into the apartment. Christopher puts the basket on the sofa table. He puts the keys on the table and removes laundry detergent from the basket.

CHRISTOPHER: I don't mean to appear ungrateful, but you must see that since you willed me that ten million dollars, my life has become a complete and utter shambles. And I don't even have the money yet.

ROSENBERG: I wish you'd listen to me. Miriam always had the girl separate the brights from the darks. It makes a difference.

CHRISTOPHER: I know you meant well, but did you really think that Lenore would just hand over ten million dollars? (*He begins to put laundry away*)

ROSENBERG: You'll get the money. Button that top button before you put it away.

CHRISTOPHER: Mr. Rosenberg, death has given you a laissez-faire attitude. Shortly, I shall be defending myself before a grand jury. Your daughter has teams of lawyers out to discredit me. She is implacable. Rumors abound that she plans to link me to the death of Marilyn Monroe. Walter thinks that the only way I can beat a murder rap is to become a celebrity. I am a terrible interview. That reporter from the *Harrisburg Queer Weekly* said that I was the weirdest thing he'd encountered since Love Canal.

(*He crosses to desk to pick up some lengths of black fabric and a sewing box, brings the material and sewing box down left and kneels on the floor. He is pinning a hem on the fabric*)

ROSENBERG: I understand your anxiety, but think for a moment what I've been through. That long walk towards the golden, blinding light. Had I only brought Ray-Bans. And then, being reunited with all my dead relatives, each one with an ax to grind. Some serenity. You should have seen my Aunt Ida and her *verbisseneh* face, "Sy, where's the pressure cooker you promised me?" (*Under his breath*) I'll give you a pressure cooker, you b . . . (*Noticing Chris*) May I ask what you're making?

CHRISTOPHER: Slipcovers for Norma's memorial service.

ROSENBERG: The old woman next door. (*He sits in barber chair*) Now, she was old. I was taken cruelly, years before my time, but that old dame had it coming.

CHRISTOPHER: Still, she didn't deserve to die like that. I keep replaying the events over and over and I don't think I'd do anything different. The electricity was screwed up again, so I re-plugged all the extension cords. All I did was turn on the microwave and her Craft-a-matic chair flung forward, hurtling her over the credenza.

ROSENBERG: And that triggered a massive stroke. You had nothing to do with it. Not really.

CHRISTOPHER: I can't help feeling responsible. Anyway, as far as we know, she had no family. A few of us thought we'd have a small memorial service for her at the take-out place she ordered from. I thought covering the banquettes with black slipcovers would give the Szechuan Palace some much needed ambiance.

ROSENBERG: What a kid. Always with the good deeds. I had to reward you. You see, Chris, when Lenore was growing up, I used to say, "Of course, I'm not the best father. What do I know from little girls, but ah, a son! That would be different." This miracle that I've come back, don't you see, it's my second chance. (*Rising*)

CHRISTOPHER: Your what?

ROSENBERG (*sitting on coffee table*): My second chance to be the father I always wanted to be. Everything you've told me about your childhood, your parents dying so young, it breaks my heart. I wish I could have been your Dad. I would have taught you how to throw a ball. I wasn't a bad softball player. I would have taken you camping in the woods. Shown you how to pitch a tent and catch a fish.

CHRISTOPHER: Mr. Rosenberg, I appreciate your interest, but I wasn't that kind of child at all. I would have been miserable.

ROSENBERG: I'm sure you were a wonderful child. No parent couldn't have loved you.

CHRISTOPHER: I was very creative. When I was six, I started my own modern dance troupe. My big fantasy as a child was to be Susan Hayward in *I Want to Live.* How many times Polly and I would take turns going to the gas chamber. One day she'd toss the pellets, the next day I.

ROSENBERG: Christopher, I want . . . I want us to communicate.

CHRISTOPHER: But we are. We've talked so much. My uvula has never had such a workout.

ROSENBERG: A father and son should have no secrets. Christopher, you haven't always been so forthcoming.

CHRISTOPHER (*slightly embarrassed about where the conversation is going*): I must confess, I find it hard talking about myself and particularly about my sexual orientation. (*Crossing with sewing to desk*) I'm really very old-fashioned.

ROSENBERG: But I need to understand. My experience with homosexuality is so limited. I blinded myself to it. I never saw that it was all around me. My own family. When I look back now I see. My cousin Phillip. He never married. He designed women's lingerie on Seventh Avenue. Lived for thirty years with a hairdresser named Conrad. Spent six months a year in Key West. Wore a caftan one year to Rosh Hashanah. I never suspected. My Aunt Esther lived for years with a very masculine airline executive named Delores. Esther called her Dudley. My nephew Jason sells Lancôme products at Bloomingdale's. I never knew. But I have this feeling that, gay or straight, I've been sent here to help you become a man.

CHRISTOPHER (*unconsciously camp*): But, darling, I am a man. I really am. (*Suddenly, he doubles over in pain*) Ow. Oh, God.

ROSENBERG (*standing*): What's wrong?

CHRISTOPHER: I don't know. I've got stomach cramps and, oh, my head. (*Suddenly aware of something*) There's a spirit in this room.

ROSENBERG: Yes, me.

CHRISTOPHER: No, another one and it's trying to get inside me. It's a man. I'm gonna let him in.

ROSENBERG: Are you sure you should do this?

(*Christopher begins moaning and strange, hoarse sounds emerge from him. His face contorts. Finally, a loud grunt, an eerie light change and the possession is complete.*)

ROSENBERG (*almost frightened, he crosses to Christopher*): Dear god, he's being possessed by an evil spirit, a dybbuk.

(*Christopher speaks in the voice of Rosenberg's dead brother Sheldon.*)

CHRISTOPHER (*as Sheldon*): No Sy, I am not a dybbuk. It's your brother, Sheldon.

ROSENBERG: Shelly? What, are you crazy? Get out of there. Don't you hurt the boy.

CHRISTOPHER (*as Sheldon*): I'm not hurting the kid. He feels nothing. What the hell are you doing here, Sy?

ROSENBERG: I had unfinished business. The young man needed someone to guide him.

CHRISTOPHER (*as Sheldon; sarcastically*): And you're just the man for the job.

ROSENBERG: Why shouldn't I be?

CHRISTOPHER (*as Sheldon*): You're a great success. The great Wall Street *macher.*

ROSENBERG (*Crossing away*): Don't talk to me.

CHRISTOPHER (*as Sheldon*): This Christopher business is all a charade. You never change, Sy. You think you're the great giver of gifts, but it's all for yourself. Checkbook love.

ROSENBERG (*irritated*): Checkbook love? All the financial help I gave you all of our lives. Keeping your business open after the fire. Mindy's wedding. Sending your Stacey to college.

CHRISTOPHER (*as Sheldon*): A junior college.

ROSENBERG: Her SAT scores were in the single digits.

CHRISTOPHER (*as Sheldon*): She doesn't need you anymore. Stacey's going to be a great cabaret singer.

ROSENBERG: The ungrateful brat wouldn't even comp me in.

CHRISTOPHER (*as Sheldon*): With your money, you should be comped? With you, there's always a payback.

ROSENBERG: Miriam warned me you'd throw my good deeds in my face.

CHRISTOPHER (*as Sheldon; scoffing*): Miriam.

ROSENBERG: What about Miriam? Are you saying I wasn't good to my wife?

CHRISTOPHER (*as Sheldon*): It was a show marriage. She was the perfect hostess. You treated her like a professional asset, like a very efficient fax machine. I was there in the next room when she was dying. I heard her lash out at you. The invective. And now you carry on about the great idyllic marriage. You're such a phony, Sy. Come back. Face your truths, face your family.

ROSENBERG: I'm not afraid of my family. I was a beloved figure . . .

CHRISTOPHER (*as Sheldon*): Well, I've got a message from your late cousin Florence.

ROSENBERG: What's Florence got to say?

CHRISTOPHER (*as Sheldon*): Florence says, "Fuck you." You wanna hear from cousin Ruthie?

ROSENBERG: Who do you think you are, the ghost of Chanukah past?

CHRISTOPHER (*as Sheldon*): I gotta go. The kid's sending me back. (*An internal struggle*) Alright, I'm going. The kid's got some will power. Jeeze!

(*An abrupt light change. Sheldon has vanished. Christopher appears frightened and slightly disoriented. Rosenberg rushes to Chris' side*)

ROSENBERG: Chris?

CHRISTOPHER: That was horrible. I really dislike your
   brother Sheldon. I couldn't get him out. (*Holding the
   black fabric up under his chin*) I feel raped.

ROSENBERG: With Sheldon, it shouldn't be so bad. He had a
   pecker this size. (*Holds up his pinky finger*)

(*The door flies open. Polly and Walter enter with lots of shopping bags. Polly deposits hers at the barber chair, and then
flings herself on the sofa. Walter follows behind her, picking
up her bags and exiting through the archway. Rosenberg rises*)

POLLY: I am vanquished. We walked all the way from mid-
   town. My feet are as swollen as two puffed-up *brioches.*

CHRISTOPHER: Don't you think it's a bit premature to go out
   on a shopping spree? We don't have the money yet.

ROSENBERG: You'll get the money.

POLLY: Darling, I needed a new dress to wear on *The
   Wanda Wang Show.*

CHRISTOPHER: You're going on *Wanda Wang?* That's fantas-
   tic, Polly. You are the perfect talk show guest. You'll love
   Wanda Wang. I watch her every afternoon. She's so
   warm and compassionate.

WALTER (*bursting back into the room*): Polly is going to be
   sitting demurely on the sidelines. You're going to be
   Wanda's guest next Thursday.

CHRISTOPHER: Me? Talk to that awful, vicious woman?
   Have you seen how she humiliates her guests?

POLLY: Chris, stop it.

WALTER: Contrary to popular belief, it's not easy booking someone on one of these shows. This took epic *schmoozing* on my part. Polly, would you get me some zinc oxide for my lips? That's for all the ass-kissing I did.

ROSENBERG: He's a wordsmith.

CHRISTOPHER: You don't seem to understand. I am poise-deficient. My last public appearance was a disaster. In the sixth grade, I was cast in the school play, *My Fair Lady.* Opening night I was so nervous, my face swelled up like a Macy's balloon. Polly insisted on going on for me.

WALTER: That was nice of her.

CHRISTOPHER: You should have seen her Colonel Pickering. Please don't make me go on TV. I beg of you.

POLLY: I really can't take anymore of this Emily-Dickinson-Shield-Me-From-the-Limelight crap. I shall let you boys thrash it out amongst yourselves. Chris, you reject everything! I am tired of giving, giving, giving! (*Exits through archway*)

CHRISTOPHER: Honestly, I'm very touched by all the effort you've made.

WALTER: I'm not all that upset. Just for a second there, I had this feeling of total obliteration.

ROSENBERG: He's very sensitive.

WALTER: Chris, this is my gift to you. The kind of exposure you can get on *Wanda* could keep this case from going to court. Wanda's big. She's got a leg up on Oprah.

CHRISTOPHER: I would if I could, but I will fail miserably. I will be struck mute.

WALTER: Look, I'm not being completely selfless. You going on *Wanda* means a lot to me in many ways. I've never booked anyone on such an important show. Please don't make me look like an idiot and cancel. Do this for me?

CHRISTOPHER: Walter, why did you have to do this? I can't . . . I can't. And I'm not going to be bulldozed into this.

WALTER: Bulldozed? *Bulldozed?* That is a word I use when I refer to my mother, Mrs. Evelyn Zuckerman. I have spent countless hours in therapy, dealing with this issue. I really can't accept this criticism. (*Beat*) Alright, I accept this criticism. Everything I do for you is only to make myself feel important. (*Stops*) If that is true, do you know why I do that? (*Slumps on sofa arm*) To make myself feel less like an impotent, ineffectual failure. I am a third-rate press agent. The high point of my career is representing this year's Mr. Chippendales and running to Waldbaum's to buy him Gasex. Do I ever get sympathy?

CHRISTOPHER: You've got it all wrong, Walter. I'm the failure in this duo. Homeless people don't even harass me.

WALTER (*standing*): *I* have no money. I live off credit cards.

CHRISTOPHER (*taking a step*): *I* can't even get a credit card.

WALTER (*taking a step*): My life is about photographers telling me to get the hell out of the way.

CHRISTOPHER: I am a Diane Arbus photograph. I can see it hanging at the Whitney. (*Sitting, illustrating photograph*)

Gay Electrologist With One Eye Closed. (*Crossing to archway*) I should kill myself. It would make a better picture.

WALTER: Oh, you won't kill yourself. You're tough as nails. You don't need people.

CHRISTOPHER (*stopping at archway*): Oh, I don't?

WALTER: I'm the one desperately seeking affection . . . and getting kicked in the *tuchus*. I should take an overdose of Seconal.

CHRISTOPHER: I'm such a dope, I'd take an overdose of Tums and end up with a giant lump of antacid in my stomach.

ROSENBERG: Would you two stop?

WALTER: Just answer me this. What is my role in your life? Am I your pal, your lover, your fling or your publicist?

CHRISTOPHER: I don't know what I want you to be. I realize that's unfair. I can't be all things to all people: lover, brother, electrologist, ghostbuster and defendant. All I know is I've got to finish these slipcovers.

WALTER: I don't understand half of what you're saying. I've gotta get out of here. I can't stand confrontations.

CHRISTOPHER: No, no, no, no. *I'm* the one who hates confrontations. Other than Lobster Cantonese, confrontations are what you enjoy most. You just love to communicate. Why must everyone communicate?

WALTER: Don't worry about it. I'm turning off all five hundred channels. (*Exits through front door. Christopher, ut-*

terly frustrated, looks at Rosenberg and collapses on sofa.
Blackout.)

Scene Two

Panels have been pulled from both sides of the proscenium to
reveal the set of The Wanda Wang Show. *Three chairs sit in*
typical talk-show formation just left of center. The entrance, a
space between the two sets of panels, is center. Polly and
Walter are discovered center. Walter is pacing.

WALTER: I shouldn't be here. I'll just get Chris nervous.
(*Stops*)

POLLY: Darling, you must be here. You're our publicist.
You know how shy we both are. We need a spokesman.

WALTER: Polly, you shouldn't have called me and I
shouldn't have said yes.

POLLY: But, darling, this is your Napoleonic triumph. You
set this up.

WALTER: But it was the Waterloo for my relationship.
How's Chris doing?

POLLY: I told him, just a little finger down the throat and
he'll feel divine.

WALTER: How'd you get him to appear on the show?

POLLY: It wasn't so arduous, really. I have my little ways.
Anyway, darling, by his appearing on the show, it's his
way of telling you he wants to make things up. Make it

easy for him, will you? Apologize? Regret is such an attractive quality in a man.

(*Walter begins to walk away. Christopher enters. He is visibly a nervous wreck*)

CHRISTOPHER: Hello, Walter. I feel compelled to warn you about getting too close to that woman.

WALTER: Why is that?

CHRISTOPHER: She is evil. She'll go to any lengths to get what she wants.

WALTER: What did she do to get you here?

POLLY: It really doesn't bear repetition.

CHRISTOPHER: You know the doll I made out of dried yams? My favorite one?

WALTER: The one based on Gene Tierney in *Laura?*

CHRISTOPHER: She's holding it hostage and is threatening to turn it into Edward G. Robinson. I hate her. Maybe if I get the ten million dollars, she'll finally move out.

POLLY: Chris, you'll thank me for this in the end. (*Standing*) If the media finds you sympathetic, I just know Lenore will drop her lawsuit. You will be a free man and we'll be very rich.

CHRISTOPHER: I just wish I had more confidence in myself.

(*Throughout the next three speeches, all of Polly's and Wal-*

*ter's well-intentioned advice just seems to further fuel Chris'
anxieties about being on the show*)

POLLY: I have great confidence in you. Chris, this audience
   is composed of little, insignificant people with tawdry
   little lives. They'll identify with you. Just be yourself. My
   only bit of advice is not to wave your hands around.
   Come to think of it, don't use them at all. You'll seem
   effeminate.

WALTER: Polly, you're going to make him self-conscious. *My*
   only suggestion since I do know something about this,
   not that I'm being the least bit controlling, is be careful
   raising your eyebrows. Sometimes when you get excited,
   you come off like Carol Channing playing *Sunset Boule-
   vard.*

POLLY: When I've done chat shows, I've also learned not to
   tighten my mouth. Pursed lips are so unattractive. And
   whatever you do, do not lick your lips. On television, it's
   magnified a thousand times. You'll look like a gay Saint
   Bernard. (*Gasps as she sees Wanda*) Oh, there she is.
   There's our hostess, Wanda Wang.

(*Wanda Wang enters, looking over the itinerary on her clipboard. She is a very attractive and stylish Asian woman in her
late thirties. Like many flamboyant personalities, her off-cam-
era demeanor is quite different. When she's not "on," she's
really "off"*)

POLLY (*crossing to Wanda*): Hello.

WANDA (*turning abruptly*): Hello. Wanda Wang.

POLLY (*very vivacious*): Of course we'd know you. My God,
   they'd recognize your face in the middle of mainland

China. (*Suddenly aware of her* faux pas, *she cheats up and gestures introductions*) I'm Polly Lawrence. This is my brother Christopher Ladendorf and this is Chris' publicist Walter Zuckerman.

WALTER (*defensive*): I'm just handling this one appearance.

CHRISTOPHER (*equally defensive*): I won't be needing a publicist after this.

WALTER: He's remarkably self-reliant. He doesn't need anyone.

CHRISTOPHER: Especially people who insist on taking over every element . . .

WANDA (*taking control*): Hey fellas, time out! (*Turning on a dime, to Polly*) You, the sister, didn't they tell you that no family is allowed past that door and definitely no press agents.

POLLY: I realize that, but coincidentally enough, I happen to know your assistant stage manager, Bob . . .

WANDA: You've got three minutes, then vamoose. (*Brushing past all three of them*)

CHRISTOPHER: You're very different from your TV persona.

WANDA: My image is my product and I put it right back on the top shelf when I close shop.

CHRISTOPHER: Then your perkiness is just an illusion?

WANDA: My inner self, my "secret child," she's perky. On camera, I delve into the well and draw forth that hurt little girl. Therefore on television, I'm not a phony, but in a sense, more real.

VOICE OVER: One minute, Wanda.

(*Banks of light turn on as the show is being readied to begin*)

WANDA: I'm getting the signal. We're about to start. Chris' sister and flack, outta here! (*She sits in the center chair*)

POLLY (*hugging Chris*): Darling, you're going to be divine. Personality, it's in our blood.

WALTER (*pulling Polly away and exiting with her into the audience*): Polly, go. Chris, good luck.

CHRISTOPHER (*sitting in right chair*): Wanda, do you think there's time for me to run to the . . .

WANDA (*grunting fiercely and clenching her fists, staring straight out. Not unlike a quarterback*): Fuck 'em, Fuck 'em, Fuck 'em! (*She straightens up and, like Mr. Hyde, she's transformed into her familiar, warm, intensely upbeat public self*)

CHRISTOPHER: You've delved into the well, haven't you?

WANDA: You bet I have. Chris, we're gonna have fun. You're gonna look into these eyes. They're not scary eyes. And you're gonna tell me the whole truth and nothing but.

VOICE OVER: Ten seconds.

WANDA (*getting up and pointing out someone for Chris*): See that feller in that gorgeous, orange sweater? That's

Mike. He's giving me the signal to start. (*She hands off her clipboard to an unseen assistant*) Here we go. (*She stands in front of her chair*)

VOICE OVER: In five, four, three, two . . .

WANDA (*on the air; looking into the camera*): Imagine your millionaire father dies. His will is read and you learn that he's left half of his estate to an unknown gay electrologist. Do you accept or do you fight back? "Homosexuals Who Inherit Straight Bucks" today on *Wanda*.

(*Wanda's theme music plays. Chris, in a last ditch effort, gets up and tries to escape. Wanda sits. She spots him, jumps up and grabs him just before he leaves. There is a short struggle before she finally places him back in his seat and then resumes her position. Music changes to just a steady rhythmic beating sound*)

WANDA (*on the air*): Seymour Rosenberg, a wealthy widower, began seeing a young man for electrolysis. Six weeks later, Rosenberg was dead from a massive coronary, perhaps triggered by an electric shock. The day before his death, he changed his will and left ten million dollars to the young man. Will the electrologist live in luxury with Rosenberg's millions? Or will he be charged with murder and spend the rest of his days in a maximum security prison? (*The sound of a cell door closing*) With me is Christopher Ladendorf, the controversial hair remover. (*She sits. To Chris*) Were you surprised by the contents of the will? (*Christopher, true to his word, is struck mute. He is painfully aware of all the advice given by Polly and Walter. He just can't get a syllable out. Wanda coaxes him*) But, you had a very close relationship with Mr. Rosenberg.

CHRISTOPHER (*at last, able to speak, albeit tentatively*): In one sense, but, um . . . (*he inadvertently licks his lips and is, once again, totally self-conscious. In his panic, he is unable to get his tongue back into his mouth. At long last he succeeds.*) Yes, we were very good friends.

WANDA (*as if dealing with a nut case*): Yeah. How did Mr. Rosenberg first come to see you? Did he answer an ad?

CHRISTOPHER: Oh no. That's a total misconception. He fainted outside my apartment, so I helped him inside. (*His arms begin to flail*) Once there, he saw the before-and-after photos of my client, Miss Hilda Fernandez. (*He becomes aware of his hands and sits on them. Trying to get back on track, he affects a very butch demeanor and lowers his voice*) And, so, um . . . Mr. Rosenberg couldn't help but be impressed.

WANDA: I bet. Well, let's get right to another side of this. We have with us Mr. Rosenberg's daughter Lenore Stupack. (*Lenore enters to applause. She sits to Wanda's left*) Lenore, when you first heard the contents of your father's new will, what went through your head?

LENORE: Wanda, it was as if wild jackals had ripped apart my spleen. My father . . . I loved my father, Wanda. I was his little girl. (*Starting to cry*) I can't . . . it's still too soon.

WANDA (*to Chris*): Chris, I think it's impor . . .

LENORE: You live your life, go about your business and then suddenly, pow, out of the blue, you become a victim. I am a victim, Wanda. Garbed perhaps in Ultrasuede, but a victim nonetheless.

WANDA: You feel Christopher has plotted against you?

LENORE: From the get-go. From the moment my father stepped into that electrolysis parlor, this young man's had his eyes on one thing and one thing only, my father's wallet. This person has filched and plundered my father's final gift to me. And it's not the money that matters. It really isn't, Wanda. I want . . . I want my memories back. This horror has made me doubt the veracity of my most precious memories. I weep at night. I wail. I swear they can hear me down the street. "Give me back my Dad! Please return him to me!"

(The audience bursts into applause)

WANDA: Chris, I think you're losing them.

CHRISTOPHER: Evidently. I need help.

LENORE: He brought this all onto himself. Greed. That is the modus operandi in this particular scenario.

(Rosenberg enters and stands behind Christopher)

ROSENBERG: Don't let them kick you in the ass. You're wearing that magic tuxedo and, boy, do you look sharp. Get in there, kiddo.

CHRISTOPHER: Lenore, I think you should have the money.

ROSENBERG: That's not what I meant.

CHRISTOPHER: After all, you were his only child. *(To Wanda)* They were sort of on the outs, but I think had he lived, they would have patched things up. I mean, really, how angry could he have been? He left her ten million of her own.

LENORE (*to audience*): And all of you should know that ten million in today's economy is a drop in the bucket.

CHRISTOPHER: My sister would like me to have the money. She should be rich. She has fabulous clothes sense and no clothes. It's just pathetic. I'd love to see her in *haute couture* but, it's not worth it, not with all this ugliness.

WANDA: Do you have any other family besides your sister?

CHRISTOPHER: Nope. Just us.

ROSENBERG: I was always a loner.

CHRISTOPHER: That may have been why Mr. Rosenberg identified with me. He felt very alone in the world.

LENORE: I resent this implication, I really do.

WANDA (*to Chris*): Tell us about Mr. Rosenberg. From your heart.

CHRISTOPHER: I only knew him six weeks. I know that sounds bad. I never told him I loved him. I have a hard time expressing myself that way. He never told me he loved me either. But, I know he did. He thought I was wonderful. Wanda, can you have any idea what it felt like to have a stranger come into your life who thinks you're absolutely unique? You think I'm just weird, don't you?

WANDA (*to Chris*): No, I don't. I understand what you're saying very well. (*To camera*) I was a fat little Chinese girl from Oakland. But I had a teacher. An English teacher in the eighth grade, Mrs. Wu. She was the only person who would give that chubby little kid any encouragement. It certainly wasn't my mother. But, that's another show. Anything Wanda Wang has achieved is due to Mrs. Wu.

CHRISTOPHER: I always wanted a teacher like that.

WANDA (*to Chris*): Every child needs someone to tell them they're special. (*Having an apparent revelation*) Oh God. I'm going to reveal something that I've never said in public. (*To camera*) Something so private. Something I've lived with in secrecy for so many years. I have only one kidney. It was removed when I was twelve years old. Ever since, I've had to wear an elasticized corset, because my back muscles were weakened from the operation. (*Slowly breaking down in tears*) All my life, I've felt scarred and incomplete. (*To Chris*) Chris, oh yes, I know what it's like to feel different. To be alone . . . (*to camera*) alone in your little bathroom in Oakland, desperately trying to urinate. And feeling where that second kidney ought to be. To be so utterly alone. But, gosh, it feels good to finally get this out. It feels damn good. (*To Chris*) Chris, come here. (*She stands and gets him up*) Give me a hug.

(*The audience bursts into applause*)

CHRISTOPHER: I'm so glad I was here today. This is a classic *Wanda* show. Just like last season, when you revealed you'd had the chin implant.

WANDA: I'm very glad you were with me today.

(*Wanda and Chris sit back down*)

LENORE: Wanda, congratulations on your admission of your kidney problem. I just want to say that maybe I read this young man wrong. It is possible that he didn't intentionally brainwash my father.

ROSENBERG: She's up to something. She's brainy. She's a Barnard graduate.

LENORE (*to audience*): I'm trying to see both sides. It's possible that my father, in his weakened mental state, developed a fondness for his depilatory practitioner. These things happen. We live in a strange world. But is it fair to give this relationship the same . . .

CHRISTOPHER: Objection! I object. Your father was definitely not in a weakened mental state. No. He was sharp as a tack. He'd come over for a session and we'd talk for hours. Then, he sent me to the most glamorous charity ball. I was driven in a white Rolls Royce and felt like . . . I felt like Audrey Hepburn in *Sabrina*. I can't believe I just said that. It sounded so queeny but, oh, what the hell, I'll never be on TV again. (*With great giddy panache*) Who cares? (*The audience applauds*) Thank you. Now I'm going to give you a little encouragement, Wanda. I think you're every bit as good as Barbara Walters or Oprah or any of them.

LENORE: I totally agree. Wanda, you're remarkable. But back to my father's very suspicious death . . .

CHRISTOPHER (*carried away*): One kidney or no, you are no longer that ugly fat girl from Chinatown. (*The audience applauds*) Thank you

WANDA (*very vulnerable*): Oh, Chris . . .

CHRISTOPHER (*with great emotion*): You're beautiful, talented, accomplished and very, very special (*to audience*) . . . as every one of you ladies is, in your own fashion. (*To Wanda*) Now Wanda, give a hug.

(*Christopher and Wanda stand. She collapses in his arms. The audience bursts into applause. Wanda's theme music is heard. Lenore is beside herself that the show got away from her*)

LENORE: Shameless! Shameless!

CHRISTOPHER (*genuinely touched and trying to compose himself, he turns to the camera. Over theme music and applause*): I think it's time we took a commercial break. We'll be right back.

LENORE (*as lights fade*): I am the victim here. I am the victim.

(*Lights fade.*)

Scene Three

A week later. Christopher's apartment. The yam dolls have disappeared. Some knickknacks and books have been cleared away. There's a packing box on the window seat. Rosenberg is discovered down center and crossing to the desk.

ROSENBERG: That's quite a job. I see you've packed all your yam dolls. I salute your initiative, but you haven't even begun shopping for a house. That takes time.

CHRISTOPHER (*entering through archway with several books*

and crossing to window seat): I guess I'm just impatient to start my new life.

ROSENBERG: I keep reliving that TV show. You had such poise, such panache.

CHRISTOPHER (*packing books from desk*): I couldn't have done it without you.

ROSENBERG: I tell you, there are some great advantages to being invisible. I wish you could have seen Lenore's face when the D.A. told her she didn't have a leg to stand on. Lenore definitely inherited my bad temper. She was not a happy woman. Security had to forcibly evict her.

CHRISTOPHER: I hate hearing things like that.

ROSENBERG: The point is the fight is over. She's not contesting the will. Son, I've got a million ideas for us. First of all, I see a book. All about our friendship, something very personal from your point of view. Don't get anxious, Chris, I'll dictate the whole thing to you.

CHRISTOPHER: You know, I sort of see my appearance on *The Wanda Wang Show* as, well, graduation day.

ROSENBERG: I'm not following you.

CHRISTOPHER (*tentatively*): I was always under the impression that you came back to get me on my feet and you certainly have. I'm doing things these days I never dreamed of. I actually go to the movies now and I take the subway. What's left?

ROSENBERG: Are you giving me the heave ho?

CHRISTOPHER: No, not exactly. I'm so grateful for what you've done for me and I'm so proud to have been your protegé, but I think it may be time for me to go my own way.

ROSENBERG: I can't believe you're saying this. I guess I saw us as sort of a team.

CHRISTOPHER: Mr. Rosenberg, kids grow up and I'm definitely not a kid.

ROSENBERG: I agree, but not yet. Yes, you were a hit on that talk show and yes, Lenore got intimidated and dropped her lawsuit, but Chris, ten million dollars is a lot to handle. You need my advice.

CHRISTOPHER: I hired John Gerbner as my business manager.

ROSENBERG: He did well managing the Reagans' finances, but Chris your affairs are very . . .

CHRISTOPHER: Mr. Rosenberg, you have to go back.

ROSENBERG: So you've got your finances straightened out, but what about your romantic life?

CHRISTOPHER: What about it?

ROSENBERG: You've got Walter on hold. You don't know if you love him or hate him. This has nothing to do with me, but your life is still in complete upheaval.

CHRISTOPHER (*packing another box*): I don't know what to do about Walter. I want him in my life, but I'm afraid . . . Everyone I love dies. I'm a jinx.

ROSENBERG: On the basis of that lunatic statement alone, I'd say you need me at least until retirement age.

(*The intercom buzzes. Chris crosses to answer it*)

CHRISTOPHER (*into intercom*): Who is it?

WALTER (*on intercom*): It's me, Walter.

ROSENBERG: Buzz him in.

CHRISTOPHER (*he does so*): I can't believe Walter would make the first move. Hey, you did some sort of weird poltergeist thing, didn't you?

ROSENBERG: Alright, I put the idea in Walter's noggin that you'd phoned him and asked him over. Don't ask me how. It's like the riddle of the Sphinx.

(*The doorbell rings. Chris answers it. Walter stands sheepishly in the doorway*)

CHRISTOPHER: Hi.

WALTER: Hi.

CHRISTOPHER (*gesturing inside*): Please.

WALTER: Sure. (*He comes in and notices the packing boxes*)

CHRISTOPHER: Sit.

WALTER: Thanks.

CHRISTOPHER: Water?

WALTER: No.

ROSENBERG: Would one of you say a sentence with a noun and a verb?

CHRISTOPHER: Walter, I've been thinking a lot about us.

ROSENBERG: That's a little better, but get mushy. Go for broke. Forget my sensitivities.

CHRISTOPHER (*annoyed with Rosenberg*): I am trying.

WALTER: What are you trying to say?

CHRISTOPHER: I'm trying to say that . . . we're both such complicated people that it's inevitable that something would go wrong. But maybe if we made an effort to um . . . you could try to be less obnoxious and . . .

ROSENBERG: This is the way to patch things up?

CHRISTOPHER: Okay, not obnoxious. Irritating. If not irritating, annoying.

ROSENBERG: I'm jumping in.

CHRISTOPHER: Don't you come near me.

WALTER: I won't. Look, I'm tired of being Rhoda Reject.

ROSENBERG: I'm sorry. I've got to. Hold on, kiddo.

(*Rosenberg grabs Christopher by the shoulders. Chris groans. The lights change. Chris is now channeling Rosenberg. Rosenberg speaks and Christopher mouths the words like a ventriloquist's dummy*)

WALTER: Chris, are you alright?

ROSENBERG (*through Chris*): Walter Zuckerman, you plunge me into an emotional maelstrom. You are the most wonderful person, thoughtful, funny, intelligent. The greatest lover I've ever had. The technique, the passion, the stamina. Why you . . . you Hebraic sex machine.

ROSENBERG (*through Chris*): It's an absurdity for us to break up. Walter, there is an old saying, "*Es vet zich ovs-hailen fur de chasseneh.*" Loose translation, "Everything heals in time for the wedding." Catch my drift, kiddo? (*Rosenberg lets go of Chris with such force that Chris sails into Walter's lap*) Oy, I've got to stop.

WALTER: Are you okay?

CHRISTOPHER (*composing himself*): I think so.

ROSENBERG: Sorry I couldn't give you a smoother landing.

WALTER: Chris, I don't know what you're trying to say.

CHRISTOPHER (*taking Walter by the arms*): Walter, this is me now. (*Kneeling next to him*) I love you. I've always loved you. I do love you.

WALTER: Really? (*He kneels next to Chris, embracing him*) You really do? Oh God.

ROSENBERG: I feel like I've run a marathon in an open-toe pump.

WALTER: We really have to try to be more open with each other.

CHRISTOPHER: I will. I will try.

WALTER: You can tell me anything. You know I'm never judgmental.

ROSENBERG: He's a very open-minded individual.

CHRISTOPHER: There is something I've always wanted to tell you. A secret I've kept for a long time.

WALTER: You do have two kidneys, don't you?

CHRISTOPHER: Yes. I have two kidneys and a ghost named Seymour Rosenberg.

WALTER: Huh?

ROSENBERG: Not a good move, son.

CHRISTOPHER: Mr. Rosenberg is here in the room with us. I can see him, but nobody else can. We talk, we laugh, we watch TV.

WALTER: I don't believe this.

CHRISTOPHER: Why do you think I ordered the Playboy channel?

WALTER: This isn't a joke, is it?

CHRISTOPHER: No joke. He's always looking over my shoulder like a Yiddishe Jiminy Cricket.

WALTER: Chris, just now you told me you loved me. That was a very critical emotional breakthrough for you. Now is when you should really start intensive psychotherapy.

You can afford it now. But outside of the therapist's
office, please don't tell anyone about this ghost thing.

ROSENBERG: It's just you and me, kid.

(*We hear some commotion in the hall. The door bursts open.
Polly enters, followed by Wanda Wang and Lenore. Polly sees
Walter and embraces him. He stands and hugs her*)

POLLY: Walter, darling! Have you two reconciled? I desperately need to believe in romance.

(*Polly returns upstage. The three women stand in a line behind the couch*)

ROSENBERG: The Andrew Sisters from hell.

CHRISTOPHER: What are all of you doing together?

POLLY: Lunch, darling. It's extremely stimulating when
three powerful women break bread.

WANDA: My idea. I have several projects on my plate. You
know, your sister has a keen executive eye.

LENORE: And I have strong creative urges. (*Crossing to
Chris*) Chris, I have, shall we say, come to smoke the
peace pipe. For the past week, I have done a great deal
of soul-searching. I have walked through the fire and
emerged cleansed.

CHRISTOPHER: You don't hate me?

LENORE: Hate is not a word in my vocabulary. For days
after the broadcast, I lay in bed, drank very few fluids,
ate nothing save for an occasional Jenny Craig entrée. I

have starved myself into a new awareness. It wasn't easy having the press dub me "The Princess Of Greed."

WALTER: I was amazed at all the coverage you and Chris got after the show.

LENORE: Those awful paparazzi photos.

CHRISTOPHER: You're famous.

LENORE: I am famous. I'll tell you when it hit me. Leonard and I were in a cab in the Village and I guess we were around Seventh Avenue and we saw four, count 'em four, drag queens dressed . . . as *me!*

WANDA: Look, I don't have all day. I'm receiving an honorary doctorate at four. (*To Chris*) I want you and Lenore to be on my show next Thursday. "Enemies Who Bond."

CHRISTOPHER: I'm not sure we have.

LENORE: Be gracious. My image needs work.

POLLY: And there's more.

CHRISTOPHER: More?

WANDA: My staff can't even handle all the mail we received after your show. I tip my hat. You stole it right from under me. I want to create a show around you.

WALTER: What kind of show?

WANDA: It's called, "Can You Believe This?" We send Chris all over the country to rout out the weirdest, freakiest nuts ever to parade in front of a camera.

CHRISTOPHER: This is too much.

WANDA: I've got files of 'em. Witches in Milwaukee. Cannibals in Terre Haute. Chrissy, isn't it a pisser?

WALTER: I don't know. I don't think Chris should carry the whole show. He should be the comic relief. Essentially he's a humorist.

ROSENBERG: You're fortunate to have him. A good Jewish wife.

POLLY: I totally agree with Walter. Chris needs someone to play off of. Someone with a very dynamic personality and stage experience.

ROSENBERG: Her you need to watch out for. I think the show would be better if you . . .

(The whole room becomes a strategy session for Chris' new show as everyone puts in their two cents, except for Chris who seems to have been inadvertently left out)

CHRISTOPHER: Excuse me. *(No one responds)* Excuse me! *(Silence)* I don't see a co-host at all. I also don't think the show should be limited to just the grotesque. The fun would be to see me, with my particular outlook, infiltrating the Ku Klux Klan or Saddam Hussein's headquarters or the Palm Springs home of Bob and Delores Hope.

ROSENBERG: I don't see you and Hope. Tell them we'll take a meeting next week.

CHRISTOPHER: Mr. Rosenberg, this is my show.

ROSENBERG: Be careful. You're blowing my cover.

CHRISTOPHER: I don't care. Call me Barbra Streisand, but I need control.

LENORE: Back up a minute. (*Slowly rising*) Were you just conversing with my late father?

WALTER (*leaning in to Wanda*): He's just slightly unhinged, not enough to jeopardize any deal.

POLLY (*also leaning in*): He's an original.

LENORE (*crossing slowly to just left of Rosenberg*): You were talking to my father. He's in this room, isn't he? I felt a vibration last time I was here.

ROSENBERG: Put a lid on this quickly.

CHRISTOPHER: No, it's time you were outed.

WANDA: I see a classic *Wanda.*

CHRISTOPHER: Mr. Rosenberg is here.

(*The whole room gasps*)

WANDA: Like an energy field?

CHRISTOPHER: Like an agent.

ROSENBERG: I am deeply offended.

LENORE: I sensed it all along. I have done a great deal of research into the occult sciences. Oh yes, people have scoffed. (*She raises her hands to "feel" Rosenberg's vibration*) Daddy? Daddy, can you hear me?

WANDA (*countering Lenore, crossing down to just left of Rosenberg*): Chris, does Mr. Rosenberg visit you often?

CHRISTOPHER: Generally speaking, it's easier finding Mr. Rosenberg than the super in this building.

ROSENBERG: I am not moving.

LENORE: We need to make our peace. I need closure.

ROSENBERG: It's all about her. I'll be damned if I give her any peace of mind.

(*Lenore continues her search off through the archway. Fascinated, Wanda follows, sitting at the stool just below archway opening. Rosenberg also watches in amazement*)

WALTER: Chris, this whole thing is a warped fantasy of yours. Your desperate need for a father.

CHRISTOPHER: Not so desperate.

POLLY: It's not a fantasy. If anyone could see a ghost, it would be Chris. (*Disgusted, Walter retires to the Giacometti chair down left*) When we were kids, you swore you saw Mother's spirit hovering over the skunk cabbage. If Mr. Rosenberg is indeed in this room, then I want to see him. I'm an artist. I have imagination. Why shouldn't I see him?

CHRISTOPHER: Because he's my ghost. Whatever I have, you want.

LENORE (*offstage*): Daddy, we need to come to terms. Release the poisons.

POLLY (*seductively taking off her jacket*): Mr. Rosenberg, I can see why you'd prefer not to speak to Lenore, but you and I have always been simpatico. (*Crossing to cigarette box on sofa table*) Be a darling and light my cigarette.

ROSENBERG: You tell your sister that I will not be performing any parlor tricks for her amusement. (*Retreating*)

POLLY: Mr. R., have you ever snuck into my room while I was nude? I've always felt like I was being watched.

ROSENBERG: Not once. Not ever.

POLLY: Wait 'til you see what I've got in store for you tonight.

LENORE (*re-entering*): You are speaking to my father. (*Suddenly struck with an idea, she rushes to coffee table, takes off a ring and kneels*) Daddy, take my marcasite ring and make it spin like a dreidel.

WANDA (*setting the imaginary camera angle*): Push in for a close-up.

POLLY: Oh, I feel him on me. (*She appears to be thrown down on the sofa by an imaginary force*) Oh, his touch is so . . . oh, God.

(*Lenore, repulsed, turns away*)

ROSENBERG: Get her to knock it off.

CHRISTOPHER (*taunting Rosenberg*): Mr. Rosenberg, get off my sister. You should be ashamed of yourself . . .

ROSENBERG: You're as bad as she is.

POLLY (*writhing on the sofa*): I can't take it. This powerful, coursing feeling. Overwhelming, cataclysmic.

LENORE: I pray my dead mother can't hear this.

WALTER: This isn't happening.

ROSENBERG: I've never been so humiliated.

POLLY: Dear god, he's entered me!

LENORE: Daddy!!!

(*This is the final straw for Rosenberg, who lifts a large vase of roses and hurls its contents at Polly. Walter screams. Polly jumps up to get a towel. Everyone is caught up in what just happened*)

WALTER: There is a ghost! The dead walk among us!

CHRISTOPHER (*surveying the damage*): And my sofa's drenched. I really don't find this *amusant*. I really don't. (*He starts to swoon*) Ohhh. (*His body is undergoing a change. He almost falls*)

WALTER (*seeing Chris in trouble, he helps him to sit on the coffee table*): Chris, are you alright?

(*The lights change. Christopher is channeling another entity. He begins speaking in the voice of Rosenberg's dead wife, Miriam. Walter retreats*)

CHRISTOPHER (*as Miriam*): Why am I moving so quickly? It's turbulent. Now it's calming down. Much better. What am I doing in this garishly over-decorated parlor?

ROSENBERG: Miriam!

LENORE (*sitting in the Giacometti chair*): It's my mother. My mother's voice is emanating from Chris' physicality.

WANDA: He's channeling. We've done six shows on this.

LENORE: Mother, it's Lenore. Are you happy?

CHRISTOPHER (*as Miriam*): *Comme çi, comme ça.* It's not all cappuccinos and screenings of *Les Enfants Du Paradis,* but it's peaceful. Sy, it's not like you to be so quiet. Are you angry with me about something?

ROSENBERG: No, Miriam, I'm not angry with you. You're perfect. Always were. But, me, my terrible failings.

CHRISTOPHER (*as Miriam*): You've been talking to your brother Sheldon. Sy, your brother's a kook. Since when have you given anything he said credence?

ROSENBERG: He heard everything. That awful day in the hospital. He heard you vilify me. I'll never forget it. It was like a brand.

CHRISTOPHER (*as Miriam*): You listen to me, Sy. I was in excruciating pain. If I recall correctly, I died shortly afterwards. Some allowances, please. Yes, I'm sure I said terrible, violent things, but . . .

ROSENBERG: And I deserved them. I treated you as an acquisition, not as a partner. I was always playing a role:

the father, the great provider, the loving husband. It was all a sham.

CHRISTOPHER (*as Miriam*): There is a grain of truth in that. Oh yes. But, darling, there was so much more. Don't let Sheldon or any other of your *schnorring* relatives take that away from us. Remember the summers at Saranac Lake? The trip to Japan? Lenore, all of seven, taking over the tea ceremony. Believe me, the good was plentiful, bountiful. Now enough of this foolishness, come back to me.

ROSENBERG: I will soon, but I have things I need to do here.

CHRISTOPHER (*as Miriam*): Sy, you were needed and you've done good. The young man is on his way. Now leave it be.

ROSENBERG: I can't. I went away too soon. It's not just for him. I want to be here. It's not fair. I need a little more time.

CHRISTOPHER (*as Miriam*): Darling, there is no more time. You know it's not right to linger. You never knew when to leave the party. Herta Fleishmann still hasn't gotten over your antics at her Mardi Gras bash. If you truly love the young man, you will let him go. Let the living live.

ROSENBERG (*moved*): Let the living live. (*Smiling*) You always knew how to turn a phrase.

CHRISTOPHER (*as Miriam*): Now turn left and go out that door. It's remarkably simple.

ROSENBERG: I'll be with you shortly. (*To himself*) Let the living live.

CHRISTOPHER (*as Miriam*): Oh my, this crossing of the borders of the beyond is extremely taxing. *A bientôt,* dear.

ROSENBERG: Goodbye, Miriam, my love.

(*The spirit starts to leave*)

LENORE: Wait a minute. Mother, don't you have anything to say to me?

CHRISTOPHER (*as Miriam*): Lenore, you're way too thin. It's aging. Otherwise, my precious baby, I am so proud of you. Grace in defeat. It shows character.

(*The lights change. Chris is suddenly hurled out of the trance onto the floor. Polly and Walter rush to help him up*)

POLLY: Chris?

CHRISTOPHER: Quite a sensation.

WALTER: You're amazing.

WANDA: What a talent!

ROSENBERG: What a kid. What a man. I guess this is goodbye.

CHRISTOPHER: I never meant to hurt you. But you know this is the way it has to be.

ROSENBERG: You going to be okay?

CHRISTOPHER: It's funny, I suppose I've been surrounding myself with ghosts all my life. This will be the first time

I'm really alone. (*Noticing Walter, he backs up slightly and takes Walter's hand*) Although, I'm not really alone.

ROSENBERG: I feel like I'm in one of those prison pictures you like so much. Sy Rosenberg walking the last mile. Let's get it over with. (*He crosses to the doorway, followed by Chris*)

(*Walter, Polly and Wanda, totally in awe of the situation, follow en masse to the doorway. At the door, Christopher nods to Rosenberg urging him to make some sort of gesture to Lenore. Rosenberg picks a single rose up from the floor and tenderly hands it to Lenore. Everyone is rapt. Lenore closes her eyes and accepts it. She and her father have made their peace. Mr. Rosenberg returns to the doorway and looks at Christopher one last time*)

ROSENBERG: *Shalom*, kiddo. (*He throws open the door and exits. We hear the same otherworldly sound effect as when Rosenberg first arrived, followed by the faint tinkling of bells. Chris closes the door*)

LENORE: He's gone.

POLLY (*hugging Chris*): Chris, that was incredible. Think of all the fabulous dead people we can invite to parties.

CHRISTOPHER (*suddenly*): I've got an idea.

WANDA: For the show?

CHRISTOPHER: I know exactly what I must do with my ten million dollars. I don't need a new house. I'm going to need every bit of cash to build the Seymour L. Rosenberg Center for Jewish Studies.

POLLY: Have you gone mad?

CHRISTOPHER: Lenore, your father must never be forgotten.

POLLY: But all of your money?

CHRISTOPHER: Marble's expensive.

WALTER: He's flipping out.

CHRISTOPHER: It's simple. Mr. Rosenberg gave me his money and I'm giving it back to his people.

LENORE: I'm his people!

WALTER: Chris, please don't think I'm trying to take over, but you need psychiatric help. Just a little counseling.

POLLY (*following Walter*): Christopher, I know how you feel. I think it's marvelous. If you would like to convert, I will convert with you. In fact, we'll make a day of it. However, giving away all of your money . . .

CHRISTOPHER: Polly, I'm a different person now. I've made up my mind.

(*The intercom buzzes. Chris crosses to answer it*)

POLLY (*dejectedly falling onto the sofa*): Well, you don't expect me to give all my John Galianos back.

CHRISTOPHER (*into intercom*): Hello?

MALE VOICE (*on intercom*): Federal Express for Ladendorf.

CHRISTOPHER (*into intercom*): We're on the second floor. (*Buzzing him in*)

WALTER: Chris, join me in couple's therapy.

(*Chris opens the door, steps out into the hall and waits for his package*)

POLLY: Family therapy. I'll join you.

LENORE: Group therapy. I'll join you. Another hour a week can't hurt.

WANDA: All of you come on my show. It's better than therapy.

(*Christopher returns with an envelope and closes the door*)

WALTER: What is it?

CHRISTOPHER: It's from an attorney's office. Miller, Miller, Goff and Gold. (*He scans the contents of the envelope, then sits in the barber chair*) It's about Norma Leeds.

POLLY: The old witch who died across the hall? I need a drink.

CHRISTOPHER (*reading*): "Though Mrs. Leeds may have appeared destitute, she was on the contrary an extremely wealthy if eccentric woman. To reward you for your years of kindness and generosity to your neighbor, Mrs. Leeds has bequeathed to you the bulk of her estate to the sum of fifteen million dollars. Sincerely, Louis R. Miller. Be prepared for her nephew to contest."

LENORE: Whatever you're doing, keep it up.

POLLY (*wearily*): So who are we giving this money to? The Evelyn Wood School of Speed Reading?

CHRISTOPHER (*getting up*): We're giving none of this away. (*Crossing to sofa*) For one thing, we've got to move out of this dump. Wanda, it's a good thing you're here. Saves me the dime.

WANDA: I'm here for you, bud.

CHRISTOPHER: Kids, we've got another lawsuit on our hands. We're going back on TV. (*He pulls Walter onto sofa with him*) Walter, I'm going to need your help.

(*Lenore and Wanda join them. Polly perches on the sofa corner. The five of them enthusiastically plot their new strategy as the curtain falls.*)